DRIVE WITH PURPOSE

DRIVE WITH PURPOSE

Move Your Career from
Success to Significance

Bruce W. Waller

PRAISE FOR DRIVE WITH PURPOSE

"Another great read thanks to my friend, Bruce Waller. In Drive With Purpose: Move Your Career from Success to Significance, Bruce once again creates a very engaging read with incredible common-sense wisdom. Knowing Bruce, you can feel his energy and enthusiasm come through on each and every page. As Bruce shares, when shifting focus to helping others, life transforms in the most extraordinary ways. Such a great read with so many great takeaways. Bruce, thanks for taking time to share such wisdom that can help not just in business, but in life."

— **Todd Watson**, Chief Executive Officer

The Armstrong Company

"What I love most about Bruce's words is that everything applies to anyone, no matter what level or age. It doesn't matter if you're a student, a young adult trying to find your next step, or a seasoned professional looking to validate your place in life or purpose."

— **Suzanne Myers**, Chief Human Resources Officer

Arcosa

"To know Bruce Waller is to see firsthand the transformational message of this book! The philosopher Henry David Thoreau famously wrote "The mass of men lead lives of quiet desperation." Bruce shares with us, through his life and his words, how instead to lead lives of quiet significance. In a stress-filled world sometimes seemingly void of meaning, Bruce invites you to step into this blueprint, filled with practical tips and real-world examples, and decide to DRIVE your life WITH PURPOSE. Join the movement!"

— **Jimmy Taylor**, SHRM-SCP, Executive Director
DallasHR and The HRSouthwest Conference

"I had the privilege to coach Bruce during his high school years. Bruce was a fierce competitor during his playing days. He has applied that to his life and in his work. I am so impressed with his writings and the information he shares. I have used some of his writings in our pregame speeches for our football games. We invited Bruce to do an Inservice for our teachers. He did an outstanding job in his presentation. This book is another example of his insight on life and his commitment to his job by serving others in his career."

— **Mike Snyder**, CAA Athletic Director, Head Football Coach
Seminole Public Schools

DEDICATION

This book is dedicated to my grandfather, Wayland E. Causey, who died while serving our country for the US Navy during WWII, and to all the men and women who have shown me how to live with purpose and look beyond success to carve 'significance' in life's calling. Each of you have inspired me—schoolteachers, coaches, business leaders, co-workers, customers, volunteers, conference speakers, friends, and family—may you continue to stay in pursuit of life's purpose.

And to my grandchildren, Crosby and Sutton—you are significant...today, tomorrow, and forever.

CONTENTS

FOREWORD

When I was first asked to write the foreword for this book, I didn't know where to start. I wouldn't describe myself as an over-sharer, and certainly couldn't imagine providing value on what I deemed a 'self-help' book. Then I read the collection of stories that you are about to enjoy. Now I get it. The best way we can help others is to share OUR stories. Whether reassessing a career path, building a purpose-driven mindset, overcoming barriers, or simply building meaningful connections, we are drawn to the stories where we can relate. Infuse pointed guidance with relevant success stories, and you have a powerful tool to help people see the way forward.

The author and I have a unique relationship—different than most who will read this book. Bruce Waller is my father. Not only do we share many personality traits and characteristics, but I have had a front row seat to many of the stories included in this book. While Bruce is driving with purpose, I am somewhere in the car all along the way—at least for the past 38 years anyways. I've watched my father transition between many professional roles over the years, changing lanes as we were riding along. I didn't realize it at the time, but I think this helped to shape my story as I grew older. I have had many jobs in my relatively short time in the workforce, and I never felt encumbered by transitioning fields and trying something new. Maybe this was naivety of a youth navigating corporate life, not worrying about having mouths to feed, or maybe something different. Maybe I had learned through my father's journey that changing careers or priorities isn't a scary thing, but an opportunity to grow and seek the career significance for which a lot of people yearn.

Recently, I've had direct experience with pursuing significance over success. In 2012, I began a career in IT Consulting, providing sales support for an international staffing firm. For anyone who has been in a sales role, you know that success doesn't come easy or quickly. From watching my dad make a similar transition, I had firsthand knowledge that it takes several years of work before really seeing the results. With this in mind, I dug in and focused on growth rather than immediate results. Fast forward five years later, and I was recognized as one of the top producing sales managers in the company and invited to a company retreat to celebrate the year's success and receive a fancy glass trophy—just where I had hoped to be five years ago.

After the celebrations ended and it was time to get back to work, I just couldn't focus like before. Although I was doing better financially than ever before, my daily tasks and contributions seemed hollow. I was objectively successful in the role, but the significance and career fulfillment weren't there. Did I really want to continue doing the same thing year over year, regardless of the monetary benefits? I knew the answer, but the next steps would be uncomfortable in the short term. So, being my father's son, what did I do? I changed lanes and took a temporary pay cut for a new position in a field that was really interesting to me. Cut to today, five years later, and it was one of the best career decisions I've ever made.

As you'll read in the coming chapters, self-awareness and reflections are huge drivers in establishing purpose for yourself. If something feels off, or you don't feel like you are where you need to be, listen to those feelings. More often than not, you are trying to tell yourself something. Listen! Self-awareness and reflection lead to new ideas, which lead to new possibilities and opportunities for finding the purpose we crave. I hope this book resonates with you as it did with me, and it helps to guide you in the pursuit of purpose.

Enjoy!

Adam Waller

INTRODUCTION
Success vs. Significance

"The key to life is not accumulation; it's contribution." — Stephen Covey

Bowling captivated me throughout my youth, fueling dreams of one day having major success in the sport as a teenager. At age 19, I achieved my first perfect 300 game, and I repeated this pinnacle performance ten more times over the years. I also racked up multiple 800 series awards and was honored as the President of the Southwest Bowling Proprietors in Oklahoma at the age of 25. To anyone on the outside looking in, I was experiencing success, and my journey was just beginning.

After graduating from college at the University of Central Oklahoma, it seemed inevitable that I would forge a career in the bowling industry. Yet, as I tried to balance amateur bowling, managing my parents' bowling center, and my own family life, the tournament bowler's lifestyle became increasingly challenging. While my wife worked as a teacher during the day and cared for our children, I worked most nights and spent most of my weekends working at the center or traveling to bowling tournaments. I was stretched thin, and the road to success I was on began to feel increasingly desolate.

At that time, I didn't recognize that I was missing alignment with my life's true priorities. I was on autopilot, chasing a version of success modeled by those I looked up to, without pausing to consider what truly mattered to me. Despite following their footsteps, fulfillment eluded me. I couldn't pinpoint why, but I was certain of one thing: I was yearning for something more, something of greater substance. I just hadn't identified what that 'more' was. It became clear that change was imperative, not just in my routine or career, but in who I aspired to be as a professional, a husband, and a father.

> **I was on autopilot, chasing a version of success modeled by those I looked up to, without pausing to consider what truly mattered to me.**

In response, I pivoted, sending out my resume and anxiously awaiting a response that never came. Interviews were elusive, leaving me feeling stuck. Eventually, I reached out to my brother about wanting to make a change and he suggested I consider a role at the moving and storage company where he was employed. It was a step down from the managerial position I held, but it represented a fresh start—a chance to reset. So, I applied, got the job, and uprooted my family from Oklahoma to Texas to begin anew.

Over the subsequent years, my career was a mix of hard-earned successes and setbacks. I ascended the corporate ladder, progressing from Operations Supervisor to Local Operations Manager, and ultimately to Senior International Manager within a prominent national corporation. During this time, I received my first President's Club award for international sales. It was a small award to put on my desk, but it meant so much to me. It meant that I was having success. It meant I was valued and looked at as a key member of the team. It meant I was on track to making more money and progressing in the organization, or so I thought.

As time passed, I found myself continuing to yearn for more and felt I had hit a ceiling, so I decided to make a move to become an operations leader at a new company. It was a chance to build and make something more happen in my career. In my new role, I worked long hours to help grow the organization into one of the best moving companies in the United States. From there, I advanced to General Manager. I worked hard to get better in every area including communication. I attended a Dale Carnegie Class after work for eight weeks and received the top award in the class for sales. This gave me great confidence and encouraged me to stay in pursuit of growth, as I felt it would lead to making more money and greater achievements. Unfortunately, I felt stifled in every area of the position and the pay was less than desired, so I made a move to another company as the General Manager, where I made significantly more money.

But still something was missing.

Desiring more autonomy and a job that was closer to home, I decided to make another career move, but this time to a sales position in the same industry. It was a huge change, both exciting and daunting at the same time. I went from overseeing and leading people to being responsible for only myself, building partnerships to sell relocation services to companies and families. I remember thinking how much harder it was than my previous jobs, but the position offered me new opportunities in terms of money, growth, and job advancement.

But then, one day, a seemingly ordinary phone call redefined my entire professional outlook.

The call was from a friend, his words sparking an unexpected enthusiasm within me. He had recommended me to his banker for a move. This wasn't just any business transaction; it was a trust placed in me, a personal endorsement. Talking to the banker, I realized that despite the move being physically small—just a few pieces of bedroom furniture and boxes from Dallas to Houston—it was a monumental life event for him, involving the relocation of his elderly mother from her assisted-living facility. I was determined to make this transition seamless. I invested time, even visited the pick-up location to preempt any possible hurdles. I dedicated myself to this move, ensuring every detail was handled with care.

Previously, especially when I first embarked on my journey in the moving industry, I used to compare myself to friends who were doctors, lawyers, and coaches, and felt confined by my own perceptions of what success should look like. My mindset was one of limitations. But this move sparked a profound change in my perspective. It instilled a realization that transcended the act of moving furniture and boxes; it became about moving lives.

For the first time, I understood that my role extended beyond sales and logistics; I was facilitating care and providing peace of mind—I was in the business of helping. Ironically, the ability to help others had always been within my grasp; I had just failed to see it. And in that revelation lays a truth for all of us: regardless of our professions, we are all in the business of helping—we just have to recognize it. The day I made that realization, my career transformed from a relentless pursuit of success to a fulfilling quest for significance.

The Power of a Purpose-Driven Life

The moment I shifted my focus towards helping others, my life began to transform in the most extraordinary ways. My performance in sales soared, propelling me toward the milestone of a million dollars in revenue. I embraced exercise and personal growth with newfound vigor. Although my earnings were modest, my job satisfaction and self-concept were richer than ever.

My improved disposition did not go unnoticed by my boss, who responded by enriching my professional journey with leadership and sales literature, nudging me daily to expand my horizons and forge community connections.

Every conference I attended left me charged with inspiration, igniting a desire to make a similar impact on others. The powerful quotes I gathered became gifts of inspiration that I eagerly passed on to others, as I found myself driven by a clear sense of purpose.

I turned into an avid observer of people, noting their interactions and presence in various settings. This reflection sparked an ambition to transcend my roles at work—to be not just a manager, an employee, or a coworker, but something greater. This led to the inception of a monthly newsletter to my network to stay more connected and become a person of value, a step towards a bigger goal.

It became evident that fostering connections was not solely about professional advancement; it was about being of service to others in every conversation and collaboration.

By selectively engaging with fewer groups, my contributions became more focused and meaningful. Deep involvement with my industry and local HR associations proved to be the fertile ground where I could make a real difference, connecting authentically with those utilizing our services.

One ordinary day was marked by an extraordinary token—a convention brochure adorned with a note from our VP of Sales, envisioning me as a potential President's Club nominee. This small gesture was transformative, a genuine 'career lifter,' infusing me with confidence and a clear vision of future success. It propelled me to redouble my efforts, not just in business development but in nurturing relationships. It became evident that fostering connections was not solely about professional advancement; it was about being of service to others in every conversation and collaboration.

In time, that vision manifested into reality. Standing at The Broadmoor in Colorado Springs, I expressed my gratitude as a President's Club inductee, having attained the pinnacle of success. Yet, as the new dawn arrived, so did the realization that my quest was far from over. My drive for excellence persisted, but my yearning for significance deepened. I sought not just to excel within the company, but to be a force of positive change for others. My ambition had evolved beyond mere achievement; I was on a path to a life marked by significance.

The Inspiration Behind This Book

This book sprang to life from a profound realization: the true essence of a fulfilling career extends far beyond personal success. It's deeply rooted in serving others and building meaningful connections. This isn't just about professional achievement; it's about how enriching others' lives can profoundly enhance our own.

My journey of transformation began when I shifted my focus from business metrics to human connections. Instead of merely focusing on my company's goals, I started focusing on people, sharing impactful stories, offering practical advice, and celebrating individuals who were making a difference. But the real gamechanger was when I began the simple practice of sending personal notes to others around me. Whether congratulating someone on a milestone or offering words of encouragement, these small acts of kindness not only brought joy to others but also enriched my sense of purpose.

The feedback I received from folks along the way was tremendous, leading me to write my first book, *Find Your Lane: Change Your GPS, Change Your Career*, a lifeline to those navigating the workplace without a clear direction. That book has since become a testament to the power of impacting others positively, and a legacy that demonstrates to my children, and theirs, the profound fulfillment that comes from a career built on meaningful contributions.

Following *Find Your Lane*, I published a journal called *Milemarkers: A Five Year Journey* to help people track their everyday and write down thoughts, affirmations, gratitude, and other standout moments in life. This practice of intentional reflection, which is vital to me, highlights the significance of living each day purposefully, mindful of the ripple effect our actions have on those around us.

Zig Ziglar's wisdom, "You can have everything in life you want if you just help enough other people get what they want," perfectly encapsulates the philosophy behind my work. This belief took on a new dimension in 2020, leading to the inception of my leadership podcast amidst the global lockdown. This platform wasn't just about maintaining connections; it was a conduit for sharing, learning, and enhancing lives, including my own. It also helped me realize that our failures in life are just part of the gig.

But the biggest lesson has been about significance—living with intention, engaging in meaningful actions within the workplace and community, and appreciating the impact of 'small' acts that hold immense value to others. It's about ordinary people who operate at extraordinary levels, who anchor their days in purpose. This book is an invitation to join them, and perhaps more importantly, to join me on a quest for a purpose-driven career not just of success, but of true significance.

How This Book Can Help You

Since you've picked up this book, my hunch is you're on the hunt for more from your career. You're ready to step beyond the success you've

> **Significance lies in the small actions that swell into great impacts. It's woven through the fabric of our everyday lives.**

already achieved and reach for something more. If you're not quite sure what that 'more' looks like yet, don't worry—this book is here to clear the fog and point you in the right direction.

Often, when we think about what makes a career significant, we imagine monumental roles—like a US President, an astronaut, a surgeon, or a Nobel Peace Prize laureate. But true significance isn't confined to these towering heights. Significance lies in the small actions that swell into great impacts. It's woven through the fabric of our everyday lives.

This book delves into the transformative journey from pursuing traditional career success to seeking deeper significance in your professional life, emphasizing the importance of aligning personal values with professional goals. The book provides practical strategies for developing a purpose-driven mindset, reassessing your career path, and fostering authentic relationships through intentional networking and leadership. Additionally, it addresses overcoming common barriers to achieving significance and highlights the broader impact of personal growth on community and industry. Overall, the book aims to inspire you to pursue a career path that not only achieves success but also contributes positively to society and personal fulfillment.

Throughout my career, I've received several accolades, but the most cherished are those like the Saul Gresky Relocation Professional of the Year, the Global Mobility Top 100 Most Admired Service Providers, and the UniGroup Sales Stewardship Award—the highest honor for sales leadership at our annual convention. What makes these awards truly special is that they come from my peers, reaffirming my commitment to driving in the lane of significance and staying the course in my everyday.

We all wonder at times if we're making a difference or if we're aligned with our true selves. But, when you zero in on what's fundamentally important, life has a way of letting you know.

Living a life of significance has granted me immeasurable rewards. Even when the going gets tough, investing in others yields the greatest rewards in any career. Each day brims with gratitude. There's a certain energy that surges through me when I can uplift someone with a simple phone call or text message, or when I pass along a resume to a connection, leading to their renewed hope and inspiration. Inspiration is a two-way street—we ignite it in others, and their stories, in turn, kindle ours.

The stories of individuals driving in the lane of significance have been a source of my inspiration. Today, the collection of personal notes in my briefcase, each a testament to a moment of connection, fills me with greater pride than any of the accolades adorning my walls.

If you're feeling like you've veered off course or questioning your value, or even looking to recalibrate your career GPS, this book is your compass. It's not just about getting back on track—it's a blueprint for constructing a career rich with significance. My hope is that these pages will prompt you to switch lanes or hit the gas on your journey. I want you to enjoy reading this book as much as I enjoyed writing it, and to pass it on, perhaps to a friend (or team member) who needs a boost.

Here's to driving with purpose and steering towards not only a great career but a life brimming with significance—it's closer than you think!

CHAPTER 1

Understanding Success

"Success is not the key to happiness. Happiness is the key to success."
— Albert Schweitzer

S uccess, like beauty, is often in the eye of the beholder. Personally, it might be the joy you feel when your work aligns with your passions, the balance you maintain between your job and your personal life, or the pride that swells within you after a hard day's work.

When I wrote my first book, *Find Your Lane*, I shared a story about how I had given up on college, and left school to get married and start a family after my freshmen year. I was young and struggling with what I wanted in life. I didn't have any goals and wasn't really trying to make anything happen. I was working from paycheck to paycheck to put food on the table and pay the rent.

Several years later, my wife asked me about my plans for my life and if I had ever thought about going back to school. She got me to think about my life ahead and encouraged me to go back and finish college. Four years later, with my degree in hand, I walked across the stage feeling proud of my achievement as my family cheered me on from the crowd. We all have defining moments of success, whether it be running a 5K or finishing a half marathon. I am currently in pursuit of visiting all 50 states.

Professionally, success is often measured by titles and promotions, the salary we earn, or the recognition we receive from our peers and industries. I remember years ago, as a young manager, when my boss told me that he was going to give me a raise to increase my annual salary by 10% and move me over the $50,000 mark. I was so excited and thought I had hit the big time! I rushed home to share the news with my wife and we both celebrated. I had taken the job a few years earlier as a manager trainee for $30,000 per year and my eyes were always on the big 50. As far as I was concerned, I had achieved success!

But success is more than just a series of checkboxes on society's list of accomplishments.

Success is also a feeling, a state of being you achieve when you realize you are where you had hoped to be at a certain point in your life. Professionally, it is reaching a point where you feel a sense of mastery in your field, where others look to you for guidance, and where your decisions influence the course of your business or industry.

Yet, to fully grasp the essence of success, we must accept that it is a dynamic and evolving concept. It changes as we grow, pushing us to redefine what we strive for.

Common Measures of Career Success

Early in our careers, success may simply mean landing a job. As we progress, it could mean taking on more responsibilities or leading a team.

Take my experience, for instance. When I finished college, my dad promoted me to a management position at his bowling center. Previously, I had been an employee involved in operations, but not in a leadership role. Being appointed to Manager marked a significant milestone for me. Suddenly, I was leading people, coordinating schedules, and becoming the go-to person for questions, comments, and issues. My success was also now tied to revenue, the number of bowlers joining our leagues and events, and overall profitability.

> **Over time, success becomes less about climbing the ladder and more about the legacy we leave behind.**

Over time, success becomes less about climbing the ladder and more about the legacy we leave behind. Thus, understanding success requires an introspective look at what we value most and the impact we wish to make in our professional life and beyond.

This introspection is a common challenge in the workplace. Unlike sports, where success is measured in scores and championships, professional success requires different metrics. For a human resources (HR) professional, success might be measured through engagement scores, while a talent acquisition specialist might measure it by their recruiting numbers. In the relocation industry, a coordinator's success is often measured by their customer service scores.

Traditionally, career success has been measured by a linear progression: the positions held, the number of zeroes on one's paycheck, and the prestige of professional affiliations. Common metrics include job titles, salary increases, bonuses, and professional awards. In many industries, the size of one's office or the view from the office window have been subtle indicators of one's stature within the company.

Reflecting on my early days as a manager in the relocation industry, I recall moving into a new office building and getting my own office. That space, where I arranged my bookcase and placed business cards on my desk, where I closed the door for planning and opened it to connect with my team, epitomized my idea of success at the time.

Quantifiable achievements, such as meeting sales targets, completing projects under budget, or scaling a company's growth, also serve as benchmarks for success. We see this often when companies offer bonuses to contractors that complete a project early or perform a service with a superior rating. These are often accompanied by less tangible measures like reputation within the industry, the influence one wields in decision-making, and the network of connections one has cultivated.

However, these traditional yardsticks of success, while useful, don't always equate to fulfillment. They reflect external validation and societal benchmarks but may miss our inner sense of achievement and satisfaction. Do you ever wonder why someone leaves a job when he or she is having success? It's often because of a change in management or culture, or they no longer feel like they have the opportunity to add value or do the things that brought them joy in the workplace. Other times there is no identifiable reason, other than feeling like something is missing.

As we pivot towards a career of significance, these measures are important to acknowledge because they shape our understanding of success. But they are not the final destination. They are merely signposts along the journey toward deeper purpose and meaning in our work—a journey that enriches not just ourselves but those around us and the communities we serve.

The Benefits and Limitations of Traditional Success

The traditional markers of success aren't without their merits. Achieving a high-ranking position, for instance, often brings financial stability, a sense of security, and the means to provide for our family. Salary increments and promotions can be a testament to our hard work, skill, and dedication. They validate the hours spent mastering a craft, the late nights, the sacrifices, and the steadfast pursuit of professional goals. These milestones can also open doors to new opportunities, like attending prestigious conferences, participating in exclusive industry events, and the ability to mentor younger colleagues.

In his book, *Winning Every Day*, Hall of Fame Football Coach, Lou Holtz, shares that what he feared most throughout his career was the perils of his team being number one. Often, when we achieve our goals, we get complacent. We feel like we have achieved success. We forget about the hard work, the sacrifices, and what it took to get to that moment. Traditional success doesn't last. We hear sayings often like, "You can't win today's game from last year's home runs," or as they say in the sport of bowling, "You don't get bonus pins from winning the last tournament." And then there's the old adage, "What have you done for me lately?"

Yet, there's a flip side. These measures can also impose limitations. They tether our sense of worth to titles and material gains, which are inherently transient. The pursuit of these external symbols of success may lead to long hours at the expense of health and personal relationships. Moreover, it's easy to fall into the comparison trap, constantly measuring one's achievements against those of peers, which can lead to dissatisfaction and burnout. In focusing solely on climbing the ladder, professionals may also overlook their broader impact on the industry, community, and society.

In reality, traditional success may not equate to a sense of fulfillment or happiness. The satisfaction derived from a promotion or pay raise is often fleeting, prompting a relentless pursuit of the next goal, leaving little time for reflection on one's broader life purpose. This is where the concept of significance steps in, challenging the conventional paradigm and inviting us to look beyond the mile markers of success.

I was recently having a conversation with my friend Mark about the book by Marshall Goldsmith, *What Got You Here, Won't Get You There*. It's a story about how we all experience success throughout our careers, but being able to continue success takes effort and action to continue learning and developing our skill sets. It's the continuous learning, it's the everyday connections, and the little things each day that ultimately lead us to having continued success, and the continued success leads us to opportunities to create a life of significance

When we decide we have learned it all, we will soon regress. Therefore, we need to stay in pursuit of being a continuous learner, stay in pursuit of big goals, stay in pursuit of developing great relationships, stay in pursuit of helping others, and stay in pursuit of being a person of significance in our everyday.

> **It's a metric that isn't about climbing the corporate ladder; it's about constructing ladders for others to ascend.**

Significance and Career Fulfillment

Significance in our career shifts the focus from personal achievement to the impact we have on others. It's a metric that isn't about climbing the corporate ladder; it's about constructing ladders for others to ascend. Significance comes from the Latin word *significare*, which means "to signify" or "to mean." Thus, a career of significance is one that is meaningful not just to oneself, but also to the world.

A significant career is characterized by a legacy of influence and contribution. It's about the projects that change the way an industry operates, the mentorship that shapes the leaders of tomorrow, the innovations that challenge the status quo, and the decisions that consider both profit and social good. It's a shift from asking, "What can I achieve?" to "What can I contribute?" and "Whose lives can I touch?"

I have attended many conferences with many people who have experienced success. However, when I ask why they continue to attend conferences or volunteer and do what they do, it is never about having more success. People talk about growing their connections. They talk about continuous learning to help others. They talk about mentorship. They talk about significance.

Albert Einstein is known for saying "Try not to become a man of success, but rather try to become a man of value," which emphasizes the importance of being valuable over just being successful.

***

When your career is measured by the yardstick of significance, success becomes a byproduct, not the end goal. The aim is to create enduring value that resonates with others and makes a difference. This chapter sets the stage for a deeper dive into how you can recalibrate your professional journey towards one of significance, where fulfillment comes not just from what you've achieved, but from what you've helped others to achieve as well.

Drive With Purpose

1. *How do you currently define personal success? List the top five indicators that you believe signify you've achieved success in your career.*

2. *Reflect on a time when you reached a traditional measure of success (e.g., promotion, salary raise). How long did the satisfaction last, and what, if anything, did you seek next?*

3. *Write about an individual you consider successful outside of traditional metrics. What qualities or achievements contribute to their significance in their field or community?*

4. *Think about the concept of significance in relation to your career. What could be one action you take to shift from achieving personal milestones to creating an impact on others?*

5. *How might your definition of success evolve if you prioritize significance over traditional career milestones?*

CHAPTER 2

The Pursuit of Significance

"Success is when I add value to myself. Significance is when I add value to others." — John Maxwell

Imagine cruising along a scenic road in a dream vehicle you've diligently worked to own. That's success—it's the culmination of your hard work, determination, and strategy. It's the personal satisfaction of achieving goals and realizing ambitions.

Success is often marked by external milestones: a high-paying job, a prestigious title, a corner office, and industry awards. However, once we reach our destination, many of us find ourselves pondering, "What's next?" The view from the driver's seat, having achieved it all, can be surprisingly solitary.

Significance, on the other hand, is about the roads you pave and the passengers you bring along for the ride. It's not just about reaching the destination—it's about making the journey more meaningful and enjoyable for others. Significance is less about the accolades earned and more about the journeys enabled and the lives impacted. It's the legacy that remains long after the journey ends.

John Maxwell, a renowned leadership expert, eloquently differentiates the two: "Success is when I add value to myself. Significance is when I add value to others." In this, Maxwell captures the essence of significance. It's not just adding another accolade to your resume; it's adding chapters to the story of your life that involve enriching the narratives of others.

As we steer our careers from success to significance, we shift our focus from a self-centric view of achievement to one that is community centric. It's a transition from "What can I achieve?" to "What can I contribute?" The true measure of our career becomes not just in the assets or status we acquire, but in the contributions we make and the positive impact we have on others.

The true measure of our career becomes not just in the assets or status we acquire, but in the contributions we make and the positive impact we have on others.

Learn, Earn, and Return

One of my favorite Chinese proverbs is "To know the road ahead, ask those coming back." It's inspiring and speaks to the time I got to have lunch with and learn from Chief Human Resources Officer, Shelie Gustafson. Shelie is a people leader for a large firm in Dallas, Texas.

As we sat and talked, she shared a story with me that a friend had shared with her about different lanes or seasons of our careers and how we are always changing lanes from development to transition to transformation. As she explained, early in our careers we are developing ourselves, trying to learn to be a better employee or person in our workplace. We then transition through different roles or jobs in an attempt to find our lane, then one day we look up and find ourselves transformed into a different person because of the experiences and people we've encountered over the course of our careers. Through gratitude, we desire to give back to something bigger. We find purpose in our career and in our life.

Shelie then shared what her friend once said, "We learn, we earn, and we return." I paused to embed this phrase in my mind. It's simple, but powerful; easy, but complex. It aligns perfectly with what we all experience as we move from success to significance.

We start out in the lane of development, where we *learn* and develop our skillset. We then transition into a role that allows us to *earn* more money, more experience, and more recognition. Once we have the skill and experience, we eventually reach a point where we can *return* or give back to others. This is what I call *transformation*, and this is where you'll find the lane of significance.

When we reach the transformation phase of our career, we find true purpose. We understand the *why* behind all of our hard work and want to share it, and sharing it transforms us and makes us want to go deeper, to give more, and to help others. Development, transition, and transformation are all part of the career process and essential to moving from success to significance.

Shifting from Success to Significance

When I was younger, the concept of significance never really crossed my mind. I admired famous people on TV, but it was their success that caught my attention, not their significance. However, there was an experience at age 13 that left a lasting impression on me. During a youth rally in Ada, Oklahoma, with my high school football team, a man spoke passionately about his faith in Jesus on stage. His story struck a chord with me, and I shared it with my brother. This led to my baptism a few weeks later, a truly significant moment in my life.

Early in my career, my ambitions were vague, except for my desire to be a professional bowler. I was chasing success, aiming to carve out a name for myself in bowling by winning a title and earning substantial money. But as I began to experience life and grow into my roles as a husband and father, my perspective started to shift. I began to realize that my quest was for something deeper than awards and financial success; I was subconsciously yearning for significance, a realization that dawned on me gradually.

Not long after my transition into the relocation industry, I started listening to John Maxwell cassettes and began applying his principles to be a better leader. My brother was a member of his club and would share his tapes with me. They were inspiring and created a hunger in me to continue learning more.

Later, I got a chance to meet John Maxwell and take a picture with him during his *Failing Forward* book tour. It was then that I began to think about how great it would be to inspire millions of people like he did. But as I've since learned, you don't have to inspire millions or even thousands to make a difference in your career or your life. Touching the life of just one person can be just as significant.

That's because significance isn't grounded in things like fame and fortune. Instead, significance is found in the things we do in our everyday to connect with people and to be of help to others—even the small things. It's the few dollars we toss into the Salvation Army kettle bell during the Christmas season. It's the time we take to ask the driver of a bus or airport shuttle their name and thank them for what they do for us.

Unlike various measures of success, significance isn't a one-and-done thing or a sometimes thing; it's an everyday thing.

Unlike various measures of success, significance isn't a one-and-done thing or a sometimes thing; it's an everyday thing. Significance means being intentional about how you live, how you show up, how you work, and, most of all, who you want to be in your workplace and in your community. It's wanting more than what you can do for yourself; it's wanting to help and make a difference in the lives of others.

The Significance in Helping Others

I've always cherished the stories my parents share about their lives, particularly those about my father's journey to owning his own bowling center. It's a story that not only speaks to his passion but also to the power of mentorship and support from others.

My dad's love for bowling started in high school, spending time at Sunny Lanes, in Del City, Oklahoma, where he eventually got a job working alongside the owner, Jack James. One day, an opportunity arose when a 10-game marathon bowling tournament was announced at a nearby bowling center, Edmond Lanes. With Jack's blessing, my dad participated and won the tournament. Upon returning, he shared with Jack his dream of owning a center like Edmond Lanes. Jack's response, "Well, how bad do you want it?" sparked something in my dad. With guidance and support from Jack, my father eventually realized his dream, becoming a proprietor of Edmond Lanes, and later Tri-City Lanes and Shawnee Bowl, a position he's proudly held for more than 60 years.

Jack James, in helping my dad, extended a ladder of success to someone who harbored the same dreams he once did. His willingness to share his knowledge and experience was an act of true significance. He wasn't just running a business; he was nurturing a legacy.

This narrative illustrates how pursuing significance often leads us to help others. In doing so, we amplify the impact of our own achievements, creating ripples that can grow into waves of influence and change. Helping others isn't merely about altruism; it's a potent way to extend our influence and leave an enduring mark.

I remember once telling a friend through an email how their actions inspired me. Their reply, "When you're inspired, I'm inspired," perfectly encapsulates the ripple effect. Acknowledging how others impact us often inspires them in return, creating a cycle of positive influence and motivation.

Dr. Martin Luther King, Jr. posed a crucial question: "Life's most persistent and urgent question is, 'What are you doing for others?'" This question urges us to look beyond our own ambitions to the needs and dreams of those around us. It encourages us to see our careers as platforms for broader change, not just personal success.

As my dad's story shows, helping others can change life trajectories. It ties us to a purpose greater than ourselves, infusing our work with profound significance. This approach shifts our focus from mere success to being truly consequential. It transforms our achievements into tools for building bridges, opening doors, and creating opportunities for others.

In his book, *On Fire*, John O'Leary writes, "One life can, and always does, change the world." Jack James changed my dad's world, and similarly, you have the potential to make a significant impact on someone else's world.

In the next chapters, we'll delve into how you can weave this altruistic approach into your professional objectives, crafting a career that not only reaches for the stars but also scatters them into the lives of others, illuminating paths and igniting dreams.

Significance as a Sustainable Career goal

Choosing significance as a career goal sets you on a path that is both fulfilling and enduring. Unlike success, which can be transient and influenced by external factors like market trends and economic conditions, significance acts as a steadfast anchor, ensuring that your career remains meaningful through various seasons.

Early in my career, our company placed great emphasis on business planning sessions. This practice of meticulous planning became a cornerstone of my professional life. It wasn't just about setting business objectives; it also included personal aspirations outside of work. Effective planning hones our focus on what truly matters. It encourages us to be deliberate in our actions and provides a benchmark to measure progress over time.

In my experience, planning offers perspective, particularly during times of review. It helps to see beyond just the metrics, much like observing the trends of a stock market or the ups and downs of a sports season. Wins and losses are part of the journey, and planning keeps us grounded. It prompts us to consider all aspects of our lives, including activities, relationships, family, and more. By maintaining focus on the broader picture, our efforts and energies are channeled into areas that resonate with our goals.

I recall a year when I missed my sales target, which was initially disheartening. However, that same year, I joined the board of a volunteer organization, a move that led to significant relationships and eventually to my presidency of the organization. My wife and I also celebrated successes in our personal lives with our children. These accomplishments reminded me that significance extends beyond professional achievements; it's present in our personal lives too. Setbacks in our careers are inevitable, but having goals in diverse areas helps us look forward and stay optimistic. During my annual review, I remember thinking, "It's going to be okay. Good things are just ahead." This mindset, looking beyond mere numbers, was a source of motivation.

Significance offers a consistent direction amidst the ever-changing landscape of success.

Elizabeth McCormick, a US Army Black Hawk Helicopter Pilot Veteran, motivational keynote speaker, and friend of mine, wisely says, "Everything you do today builds your tomorrow." This statement encapsulates the essence of pursuing significance. It's like the renewable energy of your career, constantly regenerating with each positive impact you make. It's an investment in a future where your career is enriched not just by surviving but by thriving through the contributions you make to your field, your colleagues, and the community.

Significance offers a consistent direction amidst the ever-changing landscape of success. It fosters a deeper sense of achievement, not measured by short-term victories but by enduring influence. This pursuit isn't a sprint but a steady, meaningful journey forward, marking every step with purpose and each milestone with personal growth and the betterment of others.

How Significance Enhances Success

Embracing significance in your career doesn't mean abandoning success. In fact, it often amplifies the success you've already achieved. When you focus on adding value to others, not only do you build a robust network of relationships, but you also cultivate a reputation that enhances your own success.

Investing in others plants seeds for future opportunities and alliances. Your name starts to represent not just professional excellence, but also generosity and vision. This approach expands your professional influence and opens doors to new possibilities that might have remained concealed on a more self-focused path.

I experienced this firsthand at one of our company sales meetings in Memphis, Tennessee. These gatherings are always energizing, but this time something stood out. Our Board Chairman, Tom Watson, offered some invaluable advice that resonated deeply with me. He started with, "I want to share some wisdom with you today, so you might want to take some notes." He then outlined the following key principles:

1. **Live by the golden rule.** Treat everyone as you want to be treated—everyone from the President to the man or woman who sweeps the warehouse floor. Everyone! Acknowledge them and show respect.

2. **Try to make everyone around you better.** Remain humble. Show great humility.

3. **Be generous.** Whether it's in big ways or small ways, it doesn't matter. Just be generous. It will change your life!

4. **Have good manners.** Manners will take you places that ability won't.

Watson's words exemplify how integrating significance into your career isn't just about personal advancement; it's about fostering a broader impact. This approach fuels not just your own success but creates a ripple effect of opportunities and growth. It's at this juncture of aiding others and nurturing personal growth where the most authentic form of professional success lies.

Even if you're not in a high-ranking position, your insights and experiences hold value for others. The wisdom you share can have a substantial impact, creating a ripple effect of growth and improvement. It's in going beyond just living by these principles and actively sharing them that you make a real impact. Generosity and heartfelt advice can inspire others to achieve more—that's the essence of significance.

In today's world, where corporate responsibility and ethical leadership are increasingly valued, striving for significance aligns with contemporary professional standards. Companies and clients gravitate towards those who demonstrate commitment beyond their own profit margins. Thus, aiming for significance not only reflects a forward-thinking leader but also becomes a magnet for success, attracting opportunities and recognition.

***

As you progress through this book, consider the enduring power of a career built on significance. It's the GPS that guides you through every twist and turn, ensuring your path is both rewarding and resilient. And as you press on, you may find that the route marked by significance is not just the more scenic drive, but the one that leads to the most profound and satisfying destinations.

Drive With Purpose

1. *Reflect on your current career achievements. Which of these do you feel align more with traditional success, and which ones might be steppingstones toward significance?*

2. *Consider John Maxwell's quote, "Success is when I add value to myself. Significance is when I add value to others." Can you think of a time when you added value to others in your career? How did that make you feel compared to personal successes?*

3. *How does viewing significance as a sustainable career goal change your perspective on long-term career planning? What are some ways you can incorporate significance into your career roadmap?*

4. *Think about a moment when helping someone else in your career also unexpectedly advanced your own career goals. What did this experience teach you about the relationship between success and significance?*

5. *In what ways can you adjust your current career goals to balance the pursuit of success with the pursuit of significance? How might this balance benefit both your personal growth and the impact you have on others?*

CHAPTER 3

Discovering What Matters to You

"In matters of style, swim with the current. In matters of principle, stand like a rock." — Thomas Jefferson

Several years ago, I was struggling in my job and wondered if I needed to make a change. The economy was slowing down, and my business had plateaued. I was still having some success, but I was getting older and had worked at the company longer than any other in my career. I started thinking about my career long-term, wondering if it might be time to make a change to continue my career progression. It was something that weighed on me for weeks, but after thinking about why I joined the company, I finally concluded that what I needed was to lean in and commit to my role.

You see, when I originally decided to accept the job, I leaned into my WHY—why I wanted the job. I made the decision based on what was important to me and the job being in alignment with my values. I wanted autonomy in my career, and I also wanted to be surrounded by great people. When we are surrounded by great people, great things can happen. The office location was also close to my home.

So, when I began to struggle, I asked myself the same questions I asked when I first accepted the job: Did I still have autonomy and am I still surrounded by great people? The answer was YES. Seeing that my job was still aligned with my values and what mattered most to me, I decided to stay. I then stepped on the gas and accelerated in my work.

This story illustrates the importance of integrating personal values into your career. It's critical to know why you make decisions, because they will not only guide you to make the best choice early on but will continue to be the guide throughout your journey when considering a change. Had I not known my 'why' or the values that were important to me when times got tough,

Personal values are like the landmarks and signs that drivers use to navigate on a road trip—they're the fixed points that guide you toward your destination.

I wouldn't have had anything to guide me or serve as an anchor when things started to feel off track.

Personal values are like the landmarks and signs that drivers use to navigate on a road trip—they're the fixed points that guide you toward your destination. When aligned with your career, these values act like a GPS, ensuring that every turn you make leads you in the right direction.

Warren Buffett, one of the most successful investors of all time, emphasized the importance of certain key attributes when hiring: "In looking for people to hire, you look for three qualities: integrity, intelligence, and energy. And if they don't have the first, the other two will kill you." This underlines the critical role of values in our professional journey. Integrity, a core value, is prioritized even over intelligence and energy. We'll discuss integrity more in "Chapter 11: Rules of the Road."

When your career decisions are driven by your values, they become more than mere choices; they become integral parts of your journey. When your values are clear, your choices are easier in every area of your life. You feel good about your workplace, you feel good about the service you are providing, and you feel good when you tell your story. You also feel a sense of belief in the way you operate each day. Values infuse your work with purpose and fulfillment because they align with your fundamental beliefs. Just as road signs and GPS guide drivers to avoid wrong turns and dangers, your values help you navigate away from career paths that might lead to dissatisfaction or ethical conflicts.

Self-Reflection: Mapping Your Values

To identify the values that will guide your career to a place of significance, it's essential to take a step back and reflect. The following exercises are your opportunity to plot the internal coordinates that will map out your meaningful career path.

1. **Reflect on Past Experiences**: Think back to moments in your career that brought you genuine joy and satisfaction. What were the underlying factors? Perhaps it was a project that

27

positively impacted others, or a role that challenged you to grow. Write down these instances and look for common threads. These threads are what I call "learning moments" and they are usually tied to your core values.

2. **Consider Your Role Models**: Who are the people in your professional life or in the broader world whom you admire? What qualities do they possess that resonate with you? As novelist and critic Samuel Johnson once said, "The true measure of a man is how he treats someone who can do him absolutely no good." Contemplate this as you think about those you look up to and the values they live by.

3. **Visualize Your Ideal Day**: Imagine a day where you go to bed feeling a profound sense of accomplishment. What did you do that day? Who did you help? How did you feel? This visualization can shed light on the values that you associate with a fulfilling career. My sister once shared how we are great at sowing seeds, but when it's time to harvest, we forget to taste the fruit. We are so busy moving to the next, we lose track of the great work we have done. Taste the fruit and remember the feelings of joy in your days.

4. **Write Your Personal Mission Statement**: Based on your reflections, craft a mission statement for your career. This should encapsulate not only your goals but also the values that underpin them. This mission statement will act as your personal manifesto, a declaration of your career's purpose and

direction. In my phone, I include this under my goals to remind me of my commitment to be a good husband, dad, employee, and faithful servant.

5. **Ask the Five Whys**: When contemplating a value you think you hold, ask yourself "why" five times to drill down to the core reason it matters to you. This iterative questioning can help peel away the layers and reveal the fundamental beliefs at your foundation.

As you engage with these exercises, remember that the journey to a significant career is a personal and evolving one. Your values, like signposts along the road, will help ensure that every turn you take is a step towards a destination that is not only successful but deeply meaningful.

Integrating Your Values with Career and Community Impact

Once you've identified your core values, the next step is to weave them into the very fabric of your career. Aligning your career actions with your values is not just about personal gratification—it's about amplifying your contribution to those around you. Here's how you can start aligning your daily work with the broader strokes of your values:

1. **Set Value-Based Goals**: Establish career objectives that are in harmony with your values. If one of your values is innovation, set a goal to lead or contribute to a pioneering

project in your field. For a value like community, you might aim to volunteer your professional skills to a local non-profit organization. Each year, I post my goals in my notes app on my phone along with my values to ensure I stay aligned. For me, it starts with integrity and continuous improvement. I want to do the right thing and I want to continue learning each day. The more I learn, the more I can help others.

2. **Make Decision Filters**: Use your values as criteria for making decisions. When a new opportunity arises, run it through a filter of your personal values. Will this new role allow you to express your commitment to sustainability or teamwork? If not, it might not be the right turn to take. If you're considering a job change, ask yourself: Should I stay or go? What's changed since you started the journey?

3. **Advocate for Your Values**: Be a voice for your values in your workplace. Propose initiatives that reflect your values, such as a recycling program if you value environmental stewardship, or a diversity and inclusion committee if equality is one of your core beliefs.

4. **Seek Like-Minded Networks**: Surround yourself with professionals and organizations that align with your values. These connections can provide support and opportunities to engage in work that contributes both personally and societally. Years ago, I was serving on a local board and asked about our values. We knew we had them, but they were unwritten. We all

decided to create large letters and hang our values on the wall in our front office. Everyone loved them and it helped everyone feel more connected.

5. **Reflect and Adjust**: Regularly take stock of your career's alignment with your values. As you grow, your values might evolve, and your career might need to shift to stay in alignment. Continuous reflection ensures that you remain on the right path. A friend of mine once shared that "purpose is fluid." As we grow, our purpose and goals change, and we need to always be assessing where we are and where we want to go. When we do this, we drive with purpose.

By ensuring your professional life not only reflects but also champions your values, you naturally drive towards making significant contributions that resonate on a larger social scale. Your work becomes part of a broader journey, one that not only navigates the path of your own life but also helps pave the roads in your community.

Tools for Self-Exploration: Your Personal Values Workbook

Many years ago, my wife gave me a journal to capture my thoughts during my grandmother's final few months of life. I would make notes when I would talk and visit with her during the week and kept this up for several months. After she passed, I put the journal book away, only to find it while cleaning out my closet several years later. As I reflected on my notes, it moved me. It moved my thoughts and inspired me to continue writing again. What I found was it helped me think about my day, the people in my life, and what mattered most.

In 2019, I decided to create and publish a 5-year journal called *Milemarkers* to help people make notes each day. It is a way to capture a thought, an event, or a note of gratitude. Journaling is one great way to explore your thoughts and move toward action.

Now, let's put your internal exploration into action with some tools and exercises designed to deepen your understanding of your values and how they can be manifested in your career.

1. **The Day's End Reflection Journal**: At the end of each day, jot down moments when you felt your work was aligned with your values and moments when it wasn't. What actions led to those feelings? What changes can be made to improve alignment? If you don't have a personal journal, now is the time to order one. If you'd like to use my *Milemarkers* journal, you can purchase it through Amazon or Barnes & Noble.

2. **Your Career Pathway Map**: Draw a map or a timeline of your career journey so far, marking significant moments where your values were highlighted. Then, chart the path forward with planned steps that emphasize your values, like steppingstones leading you towards a future rich with purpose. I recently created a timeline in the Canva app, starting from when I began my journey until today. It's such a great reflection tool and

provides validation that you are driving your career and your life with purpose.

3. **The Role Model Reflection**: Write a letter to a role model (real or aspirational) who embodies the values you admire. Detail what it is about their path that inspires you and how you can incorporate their example into your own career journey. I did this one year after I read a book by former President George W. Bush and later received a letter back that I framed and hung in my office. It's now a treasure!

4. **The Value-Based Time Audit**: Keep a log for a week of how you spend your time at work. Then analyze how much of that time is spent on activities that align with your values. Use this to make informed adjustments to your schedule. Talk to a colleague or a friend and get their insight.

5. **The Gratitude Loop**: Every week, write down who has helped you in your career and who you've helped in return. Reflect on how these actions are tied to your values and the broader influence they may have. Then follow up by sending them a note of gratitude (see the 70/30 note challenge below.)

6. **The 70/30 Note Challenge**: In my book, *Life in the Leadership Lane*, I shared the 70/30 note challenge. This involves writing and mailing 70 notes of gratitude over a 30-day period. During week 1, write 1 note per day; week 2, write 2 notes per day; week 3, write 3 notes per day; and week 4, write 4 notes per day. When I did this, I received so many calls and emails from

the people I mailed the notes to, letting me know how special and impactful the notes were to them. Do this and you will find that the biggest impact will be made on you!

7. **Your Values, Your Story**: Begin drafting the story of your career with your values as the main characters. How have they influenced the plot? How will they direct the next chapters? Write the narrative of past and future career events with your values at the center.

***

As you engage with the tools outlined in this chapter, you'll begin to carve out a career that is both personally meaningful and societally impactful. Your career is more than a job—it's an extension of who you are and a testament to the values you hold dear.

Drive With Purpose

1. *Have you ever been at a career crossroads? How did you make your choices? Was it based on your values?*

2. *Research and capture a list of values. Write down your top 10, then reduce it to 5, then circle your top 3 and write them in your journal. When someone asks you about your values, you should be able to respond with confidence.*

3. *Look back at your list of values. What stands out most?*

4. *Does your company have values posted? How do they align with your values?*

5. *Do you have a journal or process to write each day? Consider making this a practice and start drawing your map to drive with purpose each day.*

CHAPTER 4
Building a Purpose-Driven Mindset

"Your attitude, not your aptitude, will determine your altitude." — *Zig Ziglar*

Whed I think about the importance of mindset, I am reminded of a crucial company sales meeting I attended at the start of the COVID pandemic. It was just days after the sports world had paused their seasons, and the whole country was bracing for COVID's impact.

When I arrived at the meeting, there was a sense of unease in the air, but I was determined to keep a *neutral mindset*. If you're not familiar with this concept, the neutral mindset is about keeping your thoughts clear of judgments, staying grounded in what's happening right now, and what can be done in the present moment.

Attending the meeting were several other sales executives, each responsible for a different department. As my boss went around the table, he addressed the burning question in everyone's mind: What does this COVID pandemic mean for us? He told the residential group they would be okay but would need to lean into our virtual survey platform to better serve our customers. Next, he assured the commercial moving folks that they would also continue to be important, as companies would need help moving desks and furniture to comply with social distancing policies. Then he looked at me and said, "It might be a long road for you, Bruce." Wait—what?

The moment I heard those words, my neutral mindset abandoned ship, and a wave of uncertainty came flooding in. A long road? What did that even mean? I'm an optimist, but I'm also a realist. And at that moment, things got very real—so real that I felt the need to check myself for injuries as I slipped off my peak and tumbled down into the valley.

I looked around the table at all the sales executives and thought, "Is this really happening?" My mind immediately went back to the year 2008 when the real estate market crashed, and people stopped moving. It was the one time I thought about quitting the industry and finding a new job that would pay my bills. I just couldn't believe I might be facing the same downfall after building so much momentum over the last 10 years. I had moved from an entry level salesperson to now representing the company as a vice president, managing and facilitating some of our largest clients. I had invested everything into this career and now I was seeing the potential destruction.

On my drive home that day, with everything I needed to start working from home, I began to think back on my career and the other times I had found myself in a valley. But none of them compared to the one I had found myself in now. Like the rest of the world, I had never experienced a pandemic before. I was in unfamiliar terrain. It was a pivotal moment in my career—an unexpected detour that was going to require some rerouting. There was just one problem—I had no idea which direction to go.

Over the next few days, I reached out to clients and friends to let them know I was thinking about them. I spent considerable time in my home office contemplating the next few months. Initially, I dreaded the impact on my sales figures, but as time passed, I managed to shift my mindset and focus on immediate actions.

Realizing the need to stay visible and connected despite social and office gatherings being cancelled, I sought ways to remain engaged and informed. I joined a Facebook learning module led by sales leader Jeffrey Gitomer, which also included my friend Beth Jee. After connecting to discuss the course, Beth and I decided to have a weekly call every Friday morning to discuss sales strategies, life, and ways to serve others during these challenging times.

It was those conversations with Beth that helped me to think beyond the usual relocation services and ponder what else people might need. Whether it was a resource or just some words of encouragement, I was determined to provide something purposeful and sustainable.

That is when I started sending daily encouraging texts, videos, and quotes to people in my network. The abundance of positive feedback I received motivated me to continue this practice, varying from a few to over a hundred messages a day. It was my way of being purposeful and saying I see you, and I am thinking of you.

That small change eventually led me to start a podcast called *Life in the Leadership Lane*. It was a way for me to look at my career through a different lens and have a purposeful conversation and connection with others each week. Instead of looking at my sales results each month and asking the question, "What am I producing?" I began to ask, "What am I sowing? What can I plant and cultivate over the next few months?" Fast forward a few years and over 180 podcasts later, not only did I manage to keep my job at Armstrong, but I managed to have some of my best sales years ever. I also published a new book, *Life in the Leadership Lane*. My podcast is also going strong, growing from just a few family members and friends as followers to now being listened to in 55 countries with 50,000 downloads and counting. In addition, I am now an active volunteer among various organizations on both a professional and personal level. In essence, I am driving in the lane of significance—a lane like no other.

As I reflect on the journey that began with that pivotal sales meeting at the onset of the COVID pandemic, the profound impact of a purpose-driven mindset becomes strikingly clear. The uncertainty and upheaval of those times, mirrored in the daunting words of my boss, forced me to confront my fears and rethink my approach. It wasn't just about maintaining a neutral, judgment-free mindset anymore; it was about actively seeking ways to be of service and finding meaning amid chaos. The steps I took thereafter—reaching out with supportive messages, engaging in enriching conversations, and starting a podcast—were not just strategies for professional survival. They were manifestations of a deeper shift towards a purpose-driven life.

My journey reinforces that success is not just about what we achieve, but also about what we contribute. It's about sowing seeds of positivity and growth, not just in our careers but in the lives of others. My story is a testament to the transformative power of mindset—a reminder that when we choose to drive in the lane of purpose, we navigate not just our own paths, but also light the way for others.

> **When challenges appear, keeping a purpose-driven mindset can help you to see beyond the challenge, to see the possibilities.**

When challenges appear, keeping a purpose-driven mindset can help you to see beyond the challenge, to see the possibilities. While it may also bring a certain level of fear and doubt, it also provides a source of strength to help us get through the moment. It brings focus to our values, and as you've learned, our values can help guide us and make better choices during difficult times.

When we focus solely on success, the pressure can be overwhelming. This is evident in business professionals who constantly travel, often at the expense of valuable family time. While every achievement has its price, true value can be found in the lane of significance.

The Bedrock of Significance: Cultivating the Right Mindset

Your mindset is the lens through which you view your career and the world. It is the mental foundation upon which all your actions are built. A purpose-driven mindset is essential when you're aiming for significance, as it focuses not just on what you accomplish, but also on the impact and legacy you leave behind.

The importance of mindset in the pursuit of significance cannot be overstated. Carol S. Dweck, a pioneering researcher in the field of motivation, teaches us through her concept of the "growth mindset" that the way we think about our abilities and potential can profoundly affect our success. When applied to the pursuit of significance, this mindset emphasizes the belief that you can grow and change through application and experience, which is essential when you're aiming to make a lasting impact.

When your mindset is geared towards purpose, you're not just traveling through your career; you're embarking on a quest.

When your mindset is geared towards purpose, you're not just traveling through your career; you're embarking on a quest. Each challenge becomes an opportunity to enrich your journey and contribute to those around you. This fundamental shift in thinking is vital for transforming mere jobs into occupations filled with intention and meaning.

To set out on this journey towards significance, consider mindset as the key to the ignition. Here are some ways to develop a mindset of growth and purpose:

1. **Embrace Lifelong Learning:** Adopt the belief that your capabilities are not fixed but can be developed over time. This open-mindedness will fuel your journey towards continuous growth and significance. One of my favorite questions to help me keep a continuous growth mindset is "How far can I go?" It comes from an inspirational leader, Jesse Itzler. He is a businessman, motivational speaker, author, and ultra-marathon athlete. He once said that growth mindset starts with asking the right questions. Instead of saying, "We did it," or "We finally made it," start by asking, "How far can I go?" That will move your thinking to another place—a place of growth. So, ask yourself, "How far can I go after I . . .?"

   - get certified
   - get promoted
   - donate to a charity
   - make a policy change
   - develop a leadership program
   - run a 5k
   - start volunteering
   - [*fill in the blank*].

43

When I started my podcast, I wanted to connect with high performers, I wanted to learn from them and stay visible in my industry. I didn't think about 100 or 200 podcast episodes. I just thought about the *next* one. But now it's time for me to ask myself, "How far can I go?" I want to challenge you to ask yourself this same question.

2. **View Challenges as Opportunities:** When faced with obstacles, see them as chances to learn and deepen your impact. By reframing challenges as opportunities, you encourage a mindset that looks for value in every situation.

I once heard a story about a professional golfer who had a great mindset. Whenever he had a bad hole, he would smile and say, "That's why they play 18 holes." It didn't bother him. He knows there are good holes and sometimes things won't go as hoped or expected. You see, many times when we walk up to hit our next shot, we may not have a good angle. Other times we might be in just the right place to make a clean hit. We can approach each situation as a challenge, or we can approach it as an opportunity to do something special, just like when a player hits an unbelievable shot straight through the trees or out of a sandpit and right into the hole.

It's the same way in life—we all can welcome our next moment, our next call, or our next meeting or conversation to create something meaningful. When we develop this mindset, it helps us to see past the impossible and identify the path to significance.

3. **Prioritize Service Over Recognition:** Shift your goal from gaining recognition to serving others. This can help align your career with a broader purpose and foster a more significant impact. When you focus on service rather than seeking recognition, you engage in a profound shift in mindset that elevates your professional and personal interactions. This approach encourages you to look beyond the immediate scope

By prioritizing service, you contribute to a culture of generosity and compassion in the workplace, which can inspire others to follow suit.

of your duties and consider the broader impact of your actions. By prioritizing service, you contribute to a culture of generosity and compassion in the workplace, which can inspire others to follow suit. This creates a ripple effect, where the focus on collective well-being and support becomes the norm rather than the exception.

Moreover, centering your career around service can lead to more sustainable and fulfilling success. While recognition and accolades are often fleeting, the impact of genuine service can have lasting effects on both the recipients and the provider. Engaging in service-oriented activities builds deeper connections, fosters trust, and often leads to more meaningful professional relationships. It also cultivates a sense of purpose and fulfillment that transcends conventional measures of success. In the long run, those who prioritize service over recognition often find that recognition follows naturally, not as the goal but as a byproduct of their meaningful contributions.

4. **Practice Empathy and Active Listening:** Make a conscious effort to understand the needs and motivations of those around you. This empathy will guide your actions and decisions towards ones that support and uplift others. When you actively practice empathy, you're not only understanding someone else's perspective but also validating their experiences and feelings. This level of understanding fosters a deeper connection and trust between individuals, paving the way for more effective teamwork, problem-solving, and conflict resolution. It creates an environment where individuals feel heard and valued, which can significantly enhance collaboration and productivity.

Additionally, active listening goes beyond just hearing words; it involves fully concentrating, understanding, responding, and then remembering what is being said. This skill is crucial in identifying the underlying needs or challenges that colleagues, clients, or stakeholders may face. By honing your active listening abilities, you position yourself to respond more thoughtfully and effectively. This not only improves your interpersonal relationships but also enhances your ability to make informed decisions and provide solutions that genuinely address the concerns of those you are serving. In essence, empathy and active listening are not just tools for personal growth; they are vital components in building a service-oriented mindset that values and prioritizes the welfare and success of others.

5. **Do Things Different**: In season four of my podcast *Life in the Leadership Lane*, I was having a discussion with leadership expert, Billie Wright, about employee engagement when she brought up the words "what if." And this just stuck with me.

    "What if I do something *different?*" This is a question you can use in both your workplace and in your personal life. The hard part isn't necessarily doing something different; it's keeping the momentum when you don't see the results. It's continuing to go to the gym when you haven't seen muscle gain or weight loss. It's continuing to post on social media when you don't see likes and comments. It's continuing to record a podcast when you don't have a following.

    What if we change our perspective? What if we change our mindset and focus on what matters most? What if we change our mindset to sowing and serving? What if we change our connections? What if we get comfortable with being uncomfortable? What if we show up to learn, show up with curiosity, or just show up to that next event? What if we make that lane change? We might fail and crash, but what is the worst thing that could happen? And what if we succeed and start to create momentum? These are the types of questions that lead to the lane of significance.

Here's an example of how I put this concept to work for me. Earlier in my career, I began to struggle in my role as the General Manager at a company in Wichita Falls, Texas. I had accepted the position about six months earlier to lead their local operations division and received a significant pay increase. It was my second job change in the previous three years, so I felt some pressure to stick around to avoid being viewed as a job hopper. But something was missing. Although the job was going well, I just didn't feel engaged or committed to the role. I really wasn't going anywhere. I was just stuck. Like Groundhog Day, everything seemed the same, and I knew it was time to make a lane change (once again). So, I began the interview process and not long after that I received three different job opportunities. One was another role as a manager in a different company, one was a sales role in a different industry, and one was a sales role in the same industry but with a different company.

During my decision-making process, I knew I wanted to take the sales role in the same industry, but the money was a lot less than I was making at the time. But as I pondered over the situation, I began to ask 'what if' questions—What if I fail? Well, I could always go back to doing what I was doing. But what if I succeed? Things could turn out great for me and it could be one of the best decisions I've ever made in my life. So, I took the position.

Several weeks after I started my new job, I was offered another job managing operations, which was similar to what I had done in the past. The money would have been great, too. But I decided to pass. Why? Because I leaned into 'what if'— What if the job I had just started didn't work out? Well, I could always go back to my previous role. But what if it does work out? What if I leaned into the position and gave it my all? In the end, that's exactly what I did. And the journey has been like no other!

Finding Purpose in Your Everyday

Awhile back I was interviewed on *The Mindful Leader* podcast, hosted by David McLaughlin, Founder of Pendulum Coaching, when I was asked about a time I'd made a lane change and began to accelerate. I replied, "When I stopped managing my days and started leading my life." We are always going to be busy with work, busy with family— busy, busy, busy. But to do what matters to you, you've got to take the reins and lead your life where you want it to go, instead of the other way around. You must live with intention every day.

So how can you stop managing your days and start leading your life? Here's a good place to start:

1. **Create a routine or system to plan your calendar.** This might require getting up an hour earlier or making it a part of your weekend activity.

2. **Ask team members you work with about their experiences.** How do they approach their weekly activities and planning? The key is to find something that also aligns with work to make work feel even bigger.

3. **Show up and ask, "How can I help?"** Though it may feel hard at first, when you do it, it will get easier and easier to stay involved, as people appreciate others who serve. During my podcast interview with Kelly Simants, Senior Human Resources Consultant with Nevada HR Team, she shared some great advice about asking for "stretch assignments." This allows you to have exposure to others' areas in the organization as well as with leadership.

4. **Ask yourself some 'what if' questions.** What if you say yes to leading your life? What if you are more intentional in your everyday?

5. **Be intentional in everything you do.** Intentionality is the key to making the 'easy' truly easier and the 'hard' less difficult. Being intentional in planning, work, relationships, and everyday activities is an important approach to dealing with the complexity of tasks that seem simple on the surface. With consistent, intentional effort, you can make complex tasks manageable and achievable.

Embracing Continuous Personal Development

In February 2023, I had the honor of receiving the Sales Stewardship Award from UniGroup at our annual Learning Conference in St. Louis, Missouri. It was a complete surprise when my name was called in front of hundreds of the industry's finest. This recognition stands as one of the most special highlights of my career. Especially considering where I started—a 19-year-old husband and father with no clear direction in life.

Reflecting on my career, I consider the journey we all undertake. It's a path marked by numerous ups and downs, successes and challenges, and highs and lows. Often, we find ourselves questioning our impact or pondering if we need to make changes in our job or career path. In these moments, it's crucial to focus on the key elements that guide us to our desired destination. For me, these elements are encapsulated in the acronym **GAPS**: **G**rowth, **A**lignment, **P**urpose, and **S**ervice.

The GAPS concept is a powerful framework for developing a purpose-driven mindset and steering your career from mere success to lasting significance. Let's break down each element of the GAPS acronym.

Growth

Growth involves continuously seeking opportunities for personal and professional development. It means embracing a mindset of lifelong learning and being open to new experiences and challenges that can enhance your skills and knowledge. Part of growth is adapting to changes within your industry and role. It's about staying relevant and being able to evolve as the demands and dynamics of your career landscape shift.

Back when I was 19 and looking for a job, I had no idea where I was headed in my career or life. I didn't have any goals, so I wasn't doing anything to further my growth. I was out of alignment with my true values, I had no sense of purpose, and the only person I was serving was myself. Not because I wasn't a hard worker, I just didn't know what I wanted.

But when I made the decision to go back to school and get a college degree, I experienced growth and further embraced personal development. This helped me to better align myself with my values, which led to me finding my purpose in life, and eventually something bigger than myself—significance through service.

Action Step: Identify areas in your career where you feel stagnant and seek out resources, training, or mentorship to foster growth in those areas.

Alignment

Alignment refers to the congruence between your personal values and your career goals. It's about ensuring that your work not only meets your professional ambitions but also resonates with your core beliefs and principles. Achieving alignment also involves maintaining a healthy work-life balance, ensuring that your career doesn't overshadow other important aspects of your life.

When I began my sales career at The Armstrong Company, I wanted to succeed for many reasons. I thought if I could be successful in sales, then I could increase my income and provide more for my family. But the biggest reason why I wanted to take a sales role was *autonomy*. In fact, it was so important, I took a 50% pay cut for the opportunity, knowing there would be potential to make more through my own efforts and success. I wanted to be in control of my schedule, which allowed me to spend time doing things that mattered most to me, primarily being a husband and a father. It also opened my eyes when I realized just how hard salespeople worked to develop business opportunities.

> **When we focus only on achievement, we sometimes sacrifice the good things in life—our relationships.**

When we focus only on achievement, we sometimes sacrifice the good things in life—our relationships. But when we live in alignment with what matters most to us, we gain fulfillment that ultimately leads to achievement.

Action Step: Reflect on your personal values and assess how well they align with your current job. Consider changes that can bring greater alignment and satisfaction.

Purpose

Purpose is about finding meaning and fulfillment in what you do. It's the driving force that gives you a sense of direction and motivation beyond just financial or status gains. A purpose-driven career is focused not just on personal achievement but on the impact your work has on others and the broader community.

One of the things I enjoy about keynote speaking is sharing my perspective and answering questions when I finish. One of the more popular questions I receive each time is around finding purpose.

I often share how early in my career I was trying to find my lane, my purpose or calling, and when I found it, my life got better in all areas. But how do we find it? How do we find that connection that creates joy in our everyday?

On my podcast, *Life in the Leadership Lane,* I ask my guests the question, "When did you find your lane in your career?" I love the answers and the stories everyone shares. Some share that one big moment, while others talk about little moments over time. However, there is a common theme among them, and that's *awareness*. It's your 'why'—knowing what makes you feel inspired and what brings joy to you and others in your everyday.

For some, finding their purpose is easy, but for others, it can be very difficult. I once read that only 25% of people know their purpose. I get it. It's one of the reasons I chose to call this book *Drive With Purpose*. It takes an intentional pursuit to be purposeful in our everyday.

Some people know their purpose early on in their career and hit the gas. But it can take time for others. If this is you, here are some things you can do to point yourself in the right direction:

1. **Start where you are—this leads to *self-awareness*.** Everyone is in a different season. If you're just starting out in your career, perhaps you need to find a mentor. If you're mid-career, maybe it's time to consider a new role. If you're in the later years of your career, it might be time to expand your reach and look for ways to be of service to others.

2. **Take an assessment—this leads to *reflection*.** I enjoy assessments because it gives me a chance to look at myself through a different lens. There are many assessments available today such as the Enneagram, Myers-Briggs, StrengthsFinder, and others. The results are interesting to review, and they help create opportunities for conversations with others for feedback.

3. **Reflect and share with others—this leads to *ideas*.** Once you've performed an assessment, ask others about their experiences. This may lead to ideas that can help you create more alignment with where you want to go.

4. **Try new ideas—this leads to a world of *possibilities*.** This is where you can start building momentum. Action changes things!

5. **Look for ways to serve others—this leads to *purpose*, and purpose leads to *significance*.** No matter how small the act, the more you do for others the more purpose you'll add to your life. Keep looking through the lens of possibilities and you will see significance everywhere.

Action Step: Identify what aspects of your job make you feel most fulfilled. Think about how your work benefits others and contributes to a larger cause.

Service

Service is about using your skills, knowledge, and position to contribute positively to others. It can involve mentoring, volunteering, or any form of giving back that utilizes your professional expertise. By focusing on service, you work towards building a legacy that extends beyond your individual achievements to the lasting impact you have on others.

> **Service is about using your skills, knowledge, and position to contribute positively to others.**

One of the most important ways I've moved my career from success to significance is by giving more of myself and my time to others, not only as a leader and mentor, but as a recent supporter of two well-deserving organizations. One of those organizations is Carry The Load, which supports military veterans who died in service. The other is the

Leukemia and Lymphoma Society (LLS), whose mission is to find a cure for certain types of cancer.

While it requires some extra time to fundraise and serve with others, which is all in the sowing, the work is very rewarding. The stories and people I have met along the journey have helped change me in ways I couldn't have done on my own. Not only do they inspire me, but they also help me feel like I belong to something bigger in life.

When I first started supporting Carry The Load, I got to honor my grandfather, who died in WWII, with a storyboard through the organization's website. This online space allows families to share stories about their fallen soldiers. I was fortunate to learn about this program through my friends Brent and Yvonne Freeman, who are incredible supporters of the organization. They shared the opportunity for me to create a place to share my grandfather's name, where he served, and a summary about what happened. You can also add something a family member said or how they felt about the person. Once the board is created, it's printed and shown during the Memorial Day event in Dallas and all across the US. Brent even gave me a smaller printed version to give to my mom. She now has this framed in her home and it gives me and our entire family joy knowing we were able to do this for her. We now participate in the honorary event each year so our families can all remember the true meaning of Memorial Day. You can read my grandfather's tribute here: https://www.carrytheload .org/ tribute-wall/wayland-eugene-causey/.

Saying yes to opportunities like this has greatly deepened gratitude in me and my family. For example, when I was attending a Carry The Load reception dinner to kick off the 2023 campaign, a friend mentioned he didn't know my grandfather had died in the war, and he presented me with a gold star coin. The moment meant so much to me and my family and served as a reminder of the importance of asking, "What if?" when it comes to deciding where to devote your time. What if I hadn't shown up to participate? Not only would I have missed out on the opportunity to honor my grandfather, but also the seed of gratitude my friend planted that day, along with what is now a beautiful memory.

When I support LLS, I get to share the story of my niece who was diagnosed with leukemia as a child and, fortunately, is thriving today. Summer was just seven years old when she and her family heard the news. We have watched her walk through the journey from shaving her long black hair to her "Make A Wish" trip to watching her give back at camps after learning she was cancer-free. When I joined the board for LLS, I asked Summer about her story. Here is what she shared:

> *"I was diagnosed on July 7, 2004 with Acute Lymphoblastic Leukemia. A day that would change my life forever. Something that scared me most were watching my friends and family have such worry and tears in their eyes. Not knowing my fate. I have always hated to see pain or sadness in loved ones. I only want to cheer them up in times of need. So seeing all that*

made me want to look strong and happy for them. Something that helped me through it all was the love and support of my friends and family. Also, I got to know so many others that were going through what I had to go through and even more. Watching those survivors helped me thrive. With their sense of humor and happiness for the world around them, it helped me do the same and kept me going. I saw such love and happiness within so many other kids it was a relief and comfort for me. Giving back to others who went through what I did and just knowing so many incredible people from my diagnosis has taught me so much in my lifetime. How to love, express, give thanks, give back and to just enjoy all the beautiful moments in life.”

As you can see, cancer couldn't take away the joy in Summer, who brings joy to everyone around her. Summer is such a light and inspiration. It's a joy to serve organizations such as LLS that bring light to the darkness for so many.

When it comes to service, there are a variety of ways to serve others outside of volunteering. Here are a few ways to be of service to others:

1. **Share stories.** We can also serve by sharing our personal stories. When I share stories online, people relate and feel a sense of connection. The more vulnerable we are, the more the listener gets out of it. Your personal story might just be the light someone needs on a dark day.

2. **Be a mentor.** Mentoring can be both formal and informal. I have mentored college students in formal programs, and I have been a mentor for others informally. Mentoring can be as simple as helping someone with a report or talking through a challenge with them. That's serving; that's significance.

3. **Start a donation drive.** I work with some of the most amazing people. Recently, a couple of our team members, called "The Sunshine Committee" (because they shine so bright), decided to bring more awareness to our donation efforts by creating a donation board to display in our office that shows our annual giving as a company. They didn't have to do this, but they wanted everyone to see the impact we're making as a company. That's service; that's significance.

By focusing on Growth, Alignment, Purpose, and Service, you can cultivate a career that is not only successful but also deeply fulfilling and impactful. This GAPS framework can help guide you in creating a career that resonates with who you are and what you wish to contribute to the world.

Continuous personal development is the journey within the journey.

Stay in Pursuit

Continuous personal development is the journey within the journey. It's the internal expedition, less visible to the world, yet arguably the most vital. In this journey, we must avoid becoming too comfortable. Every new achievement is not just a resting spot but a vantage point from which to see the opportunities ahead. It is an unending ascent, driven by the desire to enhance not just our skill set but also our capacity to contribute meaningfully to the world around us. This is a journey that challenges us to stretch ourselves, to grow, and to make a bigger impact.

When I started my career helping companies relocate talent, I wasn't sure what my purpose was other than moving people's stuff. I had no idea how I could effect change in my personal life or my career. I was just trying to make enough money to support my family. *But I stayed in pursuit.* I worked on the trucks as a young manager in training (including getting certified with my commercial driver's license) then moved my way around the organization as a dispatch supervisor, relocation coordinator, and operations leader. It was challenging and required many long days.

Later I was hired to be a general manager responsible for hiring, training, and motivating talent in the workplace. It was there that I started to realize the impact people could make in the workplace. Unfortunately, I wasn't getting the support I needed to continue. *But I stayed in pursuit.* I then decided to take a leap of faith to make more impact and to have a more purposeful career when I joined The Armstrong Company as a sales and marketing leader. I took less pay and a role I hadn't experienced before, but it was where I truly found my way, my mission, and my purpose in the workplace. And I'm continuing to learn and develop both professionally and personally to this day.

The idea of continuous learning is timeless. Think of Michelangelo, who at 87 years old said, "I am still learning." This wasn't just him being modest; it was a powerful statement about the lifelong learner's credo. It means that our journey for knowledge and self-improvement never ends, and our desire to learn shouldn't fade, no matter how old we get. This mindset turns every day into a chance to learn, every problem into a lesson, and every interaction into a learning experience. For us modern-day professionals, it means staying curious in our careers and always being open to change and growth.

***

As you conclude this chapter, envision your journey of personal development not as a series of destinations but, instead, as an infinite exploration. Remember, the road to significance is built day by day, thought by thought, action by action. This commitment to continued growth will not only enhance your own life but will inevitably ripple outward, enriching the lives of those around you and elevating the work you do to a lane of profound significance.

Drive With Purpose

1. *Do you remember a time of change in which you needed to pivot? What did you do and where has it led you today?*

2. *Do you have an organization that you are passionate about? If so, are you sharing their story so others can learn more and get involved?*

3. *Do you volunteer or have you thought about volunteering? Consider making this part of your work as you stay in pursuit of significance.*

4. *What is something you can do to serve in your workplace? Maybe you are serving today and just don't realize it. Talk to others, and if you are serving, then continue driving with purpose. It's a gift! Although you may never know how much you are helping others, know that what you're doing is truly significant.*

CHAPTER 5

Reassessing Your Career Path

"The past is behind, learn from it. The future is ahead, prepare for it. The present is here, live it." — Albert Einstein

A t various junctures in our careers, it's crucial to pull over, take out the map, and reassess the route we're taking. A purpose audit provides a systematic approach to evaluate whether your career trajectory is aligned with your values and purpose. This introspection can be both enlightening and transformative, shedding light on aspects of your job that are most fulfilling and those that are lacking.

I was recently interviewing Jim Link, Chief Human Resources Officer for the Society for Human Resource Management (SHRM), on *Life in the Leadership Lane* podcast episode 139. Jim is an inspiring leader who's doing great work for HR and business community leaders. During our conversation, Jim started talking about *followership* and how "everyone needs to be known for something." Jim shared how Jack Welch, former CEO of General Electric and best-selling author, would find people to "fill the gaps" in the areas where he needed help in his business. He found them because each person was "known for something."

This got me thinking about personal branding and how we all are known for something—but do we know what that something is? When we are able to clarify, we create followership, we create inspiration, and mostly we create value for others.

My conversation with Jim Link, focusing on the concept of being "known for something," directly ties into the importance of conducting a personal audit in one's career. This process of self-evaluation is not just about introspection; it's about understanding how others perceive you and what unique value you bring to your professional sphere. Personal branding, as mentioned, is a critical part of this audit. It involves identifying your key strengths, skills, and areas of expertise that distinguish you from others. This clarity not only helps in shaping your professional identity but also in positioning yourself effectively in your career and industry.

Navigating the Self: Conducting a Purpose Audit

Understanding what you are known for, as highlighted by Jim Link and the example of Jack Welch finding people who were "known for something," is crucial for identifying your niche and potential opportunities for growth. A personal audit involves assessing your achievements, contributions, and areas of recognition. It's about pinpointing what aspects of your work resonate most with your colleagues, superiors, and the broader business community. This reflection can reveal areas where you are most effective and passionate, guiding you towards roles and projects that align with your personal brand. It also helps in identifying any gaps in your skills or knowledge that you might want to address to enhance your professional standing.

Furthermore, being known for something specific can lead to increased followership and inspiration, as mentioned in the interview. When you have a clear understanding of your personal brand, you can leverage it to create value not only for yourself but also for others. This could mean taking on leadership roles, mentoring others, or contributing to projects that benefit from your unique skills. A personal audit is not just about self-discovery; it's about harnessing your strengths in a way that maximizes

When you have a clear understanding of your personal brand, you can leverage it to create value not only for yourself but also for others.

your impact within your organization and your professional community. It's a strategic approach to career development that allows you to be intentional about the direction you want your career to take and the legacy you wish to leave.

I was recently sitting in my living room and asked my wife what I was known for. She said without hesitation, "Networking." I smiled and thought that was really insightful. Later, I asked another person and they said, "Leadership." Not long after that I received a text from a friend asking for help since I was "known for HR." Others have told me I'm known for relocating people, SHRM, and bowling!

From networking, leadership, and HR to moving people and bowling, this got me to thinking. Can we be known for too much? As I reflect, I think about how the more we are known for, the more we can help each other. When we understand what we are known for, we create opportunities in our career and in our community to help others, especially with the things that energize us. When I think of my friends and colleagues, I immediately know what I can reach out to them for— an electrician, a recruiter, a volunteer, a business leader, a speaker, a relocation resource, and more. However, if we don't understand what we're known for, then we may miss out on opportunities to help others, even when we know we can.

How narrow or wide is your focus? Do you know what you are known for? If not, then ask—ask your network, ask on social media, ask some colleagues, ask your friends. When you find out, you can begin building your career around the answers.

What Do You Want to Achieve?

Another important question to ask as part of your purpose audit is "What do I want to achieve in my career?" It's a challenging question depending on your season of life, but important to answer as early on in your career as you can. Once you decide, you can determine whether you need to change lanes or accelerate in the lane you're in.

I've changed lanes many times. Some changes were easier than others, but each change was a mile marker to keep me moving forward. I struggled when I looked back, I struggled when I was in reaction mode, I struggled when I didn't collaborate, and I struggled when I wasn't intentional. But I kept working on me. I read, I connected, I leaned in, I showed up, I learned, and I eventually figured out how to be intentional in my everyday. I am intentional in my planning, in my workplace, in my relationships, in my workouts, in my community, and in my home life. I understand how everything is connected to people, and I figured out what was most important to me on my journey—it's people. Knowing what's important brings alignment, it brings connections, and brings joy to the journey. All this keeps us moving toward significance.

Changing lanes for me has included moving our family, changing jobs, being open-minded to trying new things in my current job, changing perspectives, changing my attitude, and changing my approach to better serve others in the workplace and in my community. It also helped me understand the power of vulnerability, which drives deeper connections, which we'll discuss in a later chapter.

Today, my focus is on being a worldclass communicator, learning from others, sharing with others, and having a mindset that I'm willing to fail to succeed. This is what driving with purpose is all about. It's defining what's important to you, then moving in that direction.

Do you remember a time when you changed lanes or changed perspective to help accelerate your career? How did it help you, or are you continuing to change lanes?

Who Do You Want to Be?

Looking ahead in your career and deciding who you want to be is another effective method of assessing your career and aligning it with your purpose. As Stephen R. Covey, the author of *The 7 Habits of Highly Effective People*, advises, "Begin with the end in mind." Consider what you want your career legacy to be. What would you want your colleagues to say about your contribution? What impact would you like to have had on your field? Such questions help solidify the vision towards which your audit should steer.

One of the questions I enjoy asking my podcasts guests is "What would your 10-year-older self say to you if he or she was knocking at the door today and you got up to answer that door?" This is such a great reflection question because it allows you to look ahead and think about where you are going, dream ahead, or give your current situation perspective.

One of my favorite answers to this question was from Global Total Reward Leader Andrew Walker, during my *Life in the Leadership Lane* podcast, episode 84. When I asked Andrew the question, he responded, "Buy a boat." He said his 10-year-older self would tell him to stop thinking about when he's done working in his career and find things that bring him joy today. He shared how he would visit summer beaches in Connecticut and would see boats going back and forth and thought about how he wasn't going to wait until he retired to enjoy life. He then went on to say, "The message I would share about my 10-year-older self would be take time to smell the roses, and don't put it off—you never know what tomorrow will bring. We all work hard, and you have got to keep working hard. I'm not taking my foot off the gas, but I'm also going to give myself a little bit of grace to do some fun stuff now and again." So inspiring!

I have received many responses from guests over the past two years that have been very inspiring. I have also had times of great pause as people stopped to reflect on the question and started crying tears of gratitude. The question can be a deep reflecting point for anyone. Many guests have shared their 10-year-older self would say "stop worrying" or that "everything is going to be okay." A few have shared they would encourage themselves to continue the journey, keep the faith, or tell themselves they were on the right path, and to keep growing.

The reason this question is so powerful is because it is often the little things we do each day that bring the most movement and change. But because it's so little, it's hard to see positive daily results. We often can't see that we are making progress or impact when we get up early to go for a run, read a few pages in a book, or help a colleague or customer solve a problem. Asking this question helps us to think about our career, and more importantly our life.

In my book *Life in the Leadership Lane*, I shared my response to the question, which is: "I think my 10-year-older self would tell me that he is proud of the person I have become. He would also say, "Keep going, keep growing, keep connecting, and keep serving others."

Find Your Pitch

We often use the term *elevator pitch* to describe the experience of meeting someone in a short elevator ride and sharing what we do as a way to establish a connection with someone we've just met. But finding your pitch can also be an excellent way to assess your career and conduct a purpose audit.

Finding your pitch is a process that requires self-reflection and clarity about who you are, what you do, and why you do it.

Finding your pitch is a process that requires self-reflection and clarity about who you are, what you do, and why you do it. Writing down and practicing an elevator pitch is a practical exercise in summarizing your professional identity and goals, which is a crucial part of a purpose audit.

The concept of an elevator pitch is closely tied to personal and professional branding, which is an integral aspect of a career audit. The pitch helps in articulating your personal brand—what you are known for, your skills, and your value proposition. This aligns with the idea of understanding your professional image as part of the audit.

Conducting a purpose audit involves not only introspection but also preparing oneself for future opportunities. The strategies outlined for creating an effective elevator pitch serve this purpose. They enable individuals to present themselves confidently in various professional scenarios, be it networking events, interviews, or casual business encounters.

Being prepared for those moments also gives us more confidence in knowing what we want to say when we are asked to introduce ourselves in a meeting. First time connections can make lifelong impressions. When we personalize our story, we can also aim to inspire.

So how do you go about finding and delivering your pitch? Here are a few strategies:

1. **Write it down.** Invest a few minutes to write down who you are, who you serve, what you do, where you work or what you are looking for, and, most importantly, why you do it. It helps if you can add a problem that you can solve too, but don't get stuck here because it can sound "salesy" when you force it. Keep your pitch to two to three sentences. Example: "My name is Bruce and I work for The Armstrong Company. I'm a relocation executive and help families relocate across the U.S. and around the world. I also host a podcast and speak on the topic of leadership. What's your name and what do you do?"

2. **Practice.** We are all going to make a first impression. The question is, will it be a positive or negative one? Invest time practicing your pitch and record yourself to see how it sounds.

Share with others for perspective. The more we practice, the better the experience will be.

3. **Embrace failure.** We may be nervous at times or stumble and that's okay because that's how we learn. Remember, the more we share our story, the easier it will get in every area of our life.

4. **Remember to use the other person's name.** When we say someone's name, they pay attention and feel more valued. It also shows we are listening and that we care. If you're unsure about the name, ask them to spell it. They'll appreciate you doing this.

5. **Smile.** When we smile, we create energy and engagement. We also create an invitation for others to share a smile too. It's the first step to building trust, which is the beginning of all great connections. When we smile, we add value and create a positive impression for everyone.

Finding your pitch can not only help you better understand who you are and what you're known for, it can also help you network, engage, and create successful connections, something we'll discuss more in chapter 6.

Identifying Opportunities for Significance

Once you've conducted your purpose audit, the next step is to scout for opportunities to weave significance into your current role. This is not always about making a drastic change; often, it's about recalibrating and refining your current position.

I saw best-selling author and National Speaker Association Hall of Famer, Steve Gilliland, speak in 2012 at my first SHRM national conference in Atlanta, Georgia and remember walking away inspired. Ten years later, I got to interview him as a SHRM Influencer about his conference session "Making A Difference" at the 2022 National Conference and Expo in New Orleans. He has been speaking at SHRM for 15 years and always draws a large crowd.

As my guest on my *Life in the Leadership Lane* podcast, episode 106, Steve shared two questions that can change the game in the workplace. The first question is **"Who's on your list?"** and he challenges everyone to name five people who have made a difference in their life.

This is a great opportunity to reflect on the people who have shaped your life over your lifetime. It's also a great way to engage in a different conversation with others, go deeper, and learn more about them, not just in the workplace, but life in general.

By identifying key figures who have influenced your journey, you can understand the types of relationships that contribute to professional growth and satisfaction. This understanding can help you develop or nurture similar relationships in your current roles and inject significance into your work.

For me, it starts with my parents, then I would add my 6th grade teacher Gilman (Gil) Davis. Mr. Davis taught me the value of connecting and networking with others when I was running for 7th grade Student Council President. I remember when he shared with our class that we should vote for the person that comes up and shakes our hand and asks for our vote, as this is how you can tell if a person is genuinely interested and if he/she is willing to serve. That week, I think I shook all 100 kids' hands during recess. This is a big part of who I am today. Then I would add my brother, my wife, and John Maxwell to round out my five. They have all inspired me to be a better leader in the workplace and in my personal life.

The second question is **"Whose list are you on?"** Who is saying you made a difference in their life? When we invest in people, we get the biggest return in our career.

> ### When we invest in people, we get the biggest return in our career.

The idea of being on someone else's list as a positive influence can help you to think about how you can be more impactful in your current roles. It's a great way to reflect and understand what actions, behaviors, or contributions could make you a significant figure in someone else's career or life, reflecting on the goal of leaving a meaningful mark in your professional environment. Understanding whose list you're on also allows you to think deeper about your relationships and the legacy you wish to create in your professional life.

Reflecting on who has made a significant impact in your life, and whose life you have impacted, directly relates to assessing how your actions and presence in the workplace have been significant. This introspection can guide you to find ways to be more impactful and meaningful in your professional roles.

Other ways to add significance in the workplace include the following:

1. **Look for projects that resonate with your values or propose initiatives that can drive positive change.** This could mean spearheading a corporate social responsibility program, mentoring junior team members, or advocating for policies that promote well-being in the workplace.

2. **Think about how your role serves others.** Even the most technical jobs have a human impact. As business philosopher Peter Drucker once said, "Management is doing things right; leadership is doing the right things." This insight beckons you to lead from wherever you are in the organizational chart, to do the right things that add significance to your work.

3. **Engage with colleagues and superiors about your desire to add value in more meaningful ways.** Open discussions about your career aspirations and how they can intersect with the company's goals can often lead to the discovery of new projects and roles that are beneficial for both you and your employer.

4. **Be a lifter.** We can all lift others in many ways, from writing a personal note to remembering people's names. Recognition is

a powerful force in the workplace. Using this approach will get you on many lists during your lifetime and that's significant.

When I took my first job in Dallas, Texas, I felt a little disappointed because I felt like I wasted a degree by getting a job in the moving business. I was moving boxes and furniture thinking about others serving as doctors, teachers, and other professional careers. My perspective was out of alignment because I was focused on me. But one day the light switch flipped when I started thinking about the people I serve when they are moving. Many are excited to relocate, while others are stressed about the idea of moving to a new city. Moving is challenging and here I was with an opportunity to really make a difference for others moving on to their next journey.

Since then, I've looked not just for opportunities to encourage, but also for the people who model great service and significance. We often take for granted the little things we do each day that can make the biggest impact.

While at a recent conference in our nation's capital, I observed some of the most amazing people serving others and making tremendous impact, and what's most amazing is they all serve in different roles. From the person who gets up early to make the coffee to the folks who set up the event tables and chairs, everyone's role is important.

If you are unsure about what you're known for or how to get on someone's list, turn your focus on helping others and you'll see what I see. Every role matters in every career. All we need to do is decide who we want to be and do it with excellence—*every day.* So set your sights on serving others. In doing so, you'll not only make a difference, but you'll also end up on someone's list.

Practical Steps for Changing Lanes in Your Industry or Role

I recently read a story about a man born in Stockholm, Sweden named Alfred Bernhard Nobel. He was a man who invented dynamite to help people in building and mining. He helped reduce costs for companies that needed to drill through large rock or take out bridges for progress. But

> **Every role matters in every career. All we need to do is decide who we want to be and do it with excellence—** *every day.*

he and others also used the dynamite to make bombs, cannons, and other explosives used in wars. One day his brother Ludvig died, and the newspaper made an error and printed Alfred's obituary in the newspaper. The obituary stated that the "merchant of death" is dead and the man who became rich by finding ways to kill more people faster than ever before, died yesterday. People hated him for inventing military explosives.

Alfred read this and realized he didn't want this to be his legacy, so he changed lanes and decided that he wanted peace to be his legacy. So, Alfred started "The Nobel Peace Prize" to recognize people making significant contributions in our society. Now, that is moving from success to significance!

If you woke up today and read your obituary in the newspaper, what would it say? Would you be proud of what you accomplished or the way you made people feel? What would you like it to say? I hope mine reads something like this: "He Learned. He Loved. And He Inspired," or "He found his lane and gave others a lift along the way." Hmmm . . . I like that!

If your purpose audit reveals a need for change, consider how you might change lanes within your current industry or role. A lane change doesn't have to be a job change or a complete career overhaul; it can be a strategic shift in your current trajectory that brings your work into closer alignment with your purpose.

First, identify the transferrable skills that can be your assets in a new role or industry. Next, engage in targeted networking, connecting with individuals who are already where you aspire to be. Learn from their journey and seek advice on how to navigate the transition.

Update your professional profile to highlight your commitment to continuous growth and your desire to contribute meaningfully to your field. Remember the importance of your brand. Craft a narrative that weaves your past experience with your future aspirations, showing how your journey thus far has prepared you for this next phase.

Lastly, consider further education or certifications if they'll help bridge the gap between your current position and your desired one. Always keep in mind that a pivot is a step, not a leap. It's a deliberate, strategic move that combines foresight with the drive to align your career with your purpose.

Everything Worthwhile is Uphill

Before concluding, I think it's important to talk about those times when things don't go quite as planned in our career or life in general. If your purpose audit serves as a reminder of how you're not quite where you want to be, I encourage you to keep going and look for inspiration. Remember—mindset is everything.

There's a saying, "Everything worthwhile is uphill." And when I run into challenges, I often think about how great it will be once I get past the hurdle. Many times, it seems like it will never happen, and I can't seem to make that change or drop that thing holding me back. This is when I lean into stories. Inspirational stories of people who overcame every roadblock that stood in the way of their calling. J. K. Rowling, the author of the renowned Harry Potter books, is the perfect example.

Before becoming a published author, Rowling was divorced and endured tough times. She could barely afford to feed her baby. When she was shopping out her Harry Potter manuscript, she couldn't even afford a computer, so she typed out a 90,000-word manuscript each time to mail to publishers. The book was rejected over and over until a CEO's 8-year-old daughter read it and fell in love with it. Since then, Rowling has become the biggest seller in children's books and later founded LUMOS, a children's charity with a mission to end the institutionalization of children in orphans worldwide. Talk about moving one's career from success to significance!

Here are a few other notable stories:

- **Stephen King**: Best Selling Author was broke and struggling trying to write his first book while living in a trailer with his wife. He received 60 rejection letters before selling his first short story for $35.00.

- **Jim Carrey**: At age 14, Jim's father lost his job and his family moved into a VW van on a relative's lawn. Jim quit school and moved to LA where he would visualize being a star one day. In fact, he wrote himself a check for $10 million and put it in his wallet dated Nov 1995. He later received $10 million for the movie Dumb and Dumber.

- **Colonel (Harland) Sanders**: At age 40 after being fired from a variety of jobs, Harland started cooking roadside at a gas station in 1930 during the great depression. Over the next 10 years, he perfected his secret recipe and later drove around selling his chicken, sleeping in his car at times. He was rejected more than 1,000 times before finding a partner.

- **Shania Twain**: At age 21, Shania's mother and stepfather were killed in a head-on collision, and she put her music on hold to take care of her brothers and sisters. Once they graduated, she headed to Nashville, and she became a very famous country music star.

- **Oprah Winfrey**: Growing up, Oprah was a victim of sexual abuse by family members and a family friend. When she was 14 years old, she got pregnant and gave birth to a premature baby boy who sadly died shortly after birth. This event was a significant and painful part of Oprah's early life experiences. Not letting this hold her back, she pursued a high school diploma and later a college degree, after which she worked her way up through the ranks of television and eventually created her very own network called OWN. Oprah also created The Oprah Winfrey Foundation, which focuses on empowering women, children, families around the world, supporting education, leadership development, and other global humanitarian causes.

As you can see, all these people had roadblocks and detours in their life. We all do. But they didn't let those challenges stop them. Instead, they kept moving forward, changing lanes, and adjusting their course along the way. This is what we all can do, and it's much easier to do when your career is aligned with what matters to you.

Stories like the ones shared above can be very inspiring. And inspiration can give us momentum by providing the courage we need to pursue our goals and passions. They can also help remind us that we can do anything we want to do if we are willing to put in the work and keep the right mindset. For more inspiring stories, be sure to read the bonus chapter, "Journeys from Success to Significance." These stories are from my own personal collection, many from leaders across a variety of industries.

Even the most carefully planned career paths can lead to unexpected challenges. When your efforts seem to veer off course, lean into your 'why.' This core understanding of your purpose will be the North Star that guides you through any storm. As psychologist and Holocaust survivor Viktor Frankl noted, "Those who have a 'why' to live, can bear with almost any 'how'." When you're grounded in your purpose, you can withstand and overcome the unforeseen obstacles that may arise.

> **When your efforts seem to veer off course, lean into your 'why.' This core understanding of your purpose will be the North Star that guides you through any storm.**

***

As we wrap up this chapter, remember the words of American poet Ralph Waldo Emerson: "To be yourself in a world that is constantly trying to make you something else is the greatest accomplishment." Reassessing your career path is about staying true to who you are and aligning your work with your deepest values. It's about making incremental changes that lead to significant outcomes. It's about not just traveling on the road but paving it in such a way that your journey remains true to your destination of purpose and significance.

Drive With Purpose

1. *Have you considered a purpose audit? It's a great time to start.*

2. *What do you want to achieve? Think about your why then add to your road map.*

3. *Who do you want to be? Write down the names of people who inspire you. What are their gifts? What is something you can work on to move to the lane of significance?*

4. *What would your 10-year-older self share if he/she were knocking at your front door today? It just might be the sign you've been looking for to get to where you want to go.*

CHAPTER 6

Networking With Intention

"Much of what you become in life depends on who you choose to admire and copy." — Warren Buffet

Reflecting on my podcast interview with Kelli Valade, CEO at Denny's restaurant, I was struck by the parallels between her stories of "counter service" and my own experiences growing up in a smalltown bowling center. During our conversation, Kelli recalled the diners where she worked, the food, the people, and, most importantly, the conversations. Similarly, my memories working at my parents' bowling centers are filled with images of pool players, bowlers, and the lunch crowd from the nearby oilfield, all gathered at the snack bar counter. This wasn't just a place to eat; it was a hub of connection where people shared stories about school, sports, work, and their passions. It was a community's heart, where real conversations and relationships were forged.

These experiences underscore a vital lesson in networking with intention. In the journey of a purpose-driven career, each interaction, each story shared over a counter, or each conversation at a snack bar or coffee shop adds a meaningful layer to our professional network. Effective networking is not merely about collecting a myriad of contacts; it's about cultivating collaborative partnerships and support systems. It's the recognition that a significant career is not a solo drive, but rather a shared voyage with fellow travelers.

As we delve into this chapter, we'll explore how intentional networking can transform not just our career path, but also how we perceive and engage with the professional world around us.

> **Effective networking is not merely about collecting a myriad of contacts; it's about cultivating collaborative partnerships and support systems.**

The Art of Meaningful Networking

The role of networking in building a significant career cannot be understated. It's not merely about opening doors to opportunities, but also about the exchange of ideas, navigating challenges, and celebrating successes together. As Reid Hoffman, co-founder of LinkedIn, puts it, "No matter how brilliant your mind or strategy, if you're playing a solo game, you'll always lose out to a team." Networking is the collaborative force that keeps your career journey dynamic and progressive.

James Allen, author of *As a Man Thinketh*, shares, "There can be no progress, no achievement, without sacrifice, and a man's worldly success will be in the measure that he sacrifices." This takes me back to all the networking events I've attended during my career. Many times, they were early morning or after business hours. I wanted to just turn around and go home before I arrived, but then I'd find myself leaving the event in gratitude that I attended. I met so many people and learned so many new things. Networking events take time, they take energy, and mostly, they take an investment in wanting to genuinely learn from others.

Early in my career, I just wanted to talk about myself, and I found it difficult to connect with people, especially those in different industries. However, my career changed when I genuinely showed up to learn, to connect, to engage, and to find ways to serve others. When we do this, we connect with purpose and create significance.

To network with the goal of building a significant career is to seek out and foster relationships that are rooted in shared values and mutual respect. It's about finding those individuals who not only inspire you but are also willing to engage in the give-and-take that breeds mutual growth. It's not a transactional interaction, but a transformational one.

When I give presentations around networking, I often ask the question, "How many of you have LinkedIn?" Everyone's hand goes up. Then I ask, "How many of you have connections on LinkedIn with people you don't even know?" Everyone's hand goes back up—including mine! It's because many times we reach out to connect, but because we are not intentional, we don't follow up after the connection. It's transactional when we don't take the time to search how we can help someone and be a better resource. To be intentional, we need to invest time into building the relationship. We need to make an investment in people. This is what leads to transformation.

I have a friend that serves as a Vice President of Human Resources. He once shared a story about how he would go on LinkedIn or send an email to executives at very large organizations to see if they would give him 30 minutes of their time to network, to discuss their role, and to find out what made them successful. He shared that he might send 100 emails and only get back 5 to 10 responses. But those responses were a connection like no other. They not only shared their ideas and strategies, but they became better connected.

When we network with the intention to contribute as much as we gain, we shift the dynamic of these interactions. We create fertile ground for ideas to grow, for mentorship to thrive, and for collaborative successes to take root. This is where the groundwork for a purposeful career is laid, where the seeds of future projects and endeavors are sown. My daily routine—coffee, reviewing my day, journaling, working out, and particularly my quiet time—is deeply intertwined with this philosophy. I make it a point to connect with my network through thoughtful texts each day. This practice not only quiets my mind but also keeps me connected to what's most important in my everyday—the people in my network.

This habit of connecting during quiet moments harks back to a practice instilled in me years ago by Coach Snyder in high school football. Before each game, Coach Snyder would turn out the lights for a period of quiet time, allowing us to clear our minds and visualize our performance. This was more than just a pre-game routine; it was an exercise in forging deep connections with my teammates. I vividly recall how Reese, our running back, would whisper to each of us, checking in and expressing his support and love for the team. This experience taught me the power of quiet connection and its role in building a supportive community. It influences my current practice of reaching out to my network during my morning routine, reminding me of the value of meaningful connections and the community they create.

To form genuine connections within professional networks requires a certain level of artistry.

This daily ritual is a continuation of those lessons learned in the locker room, a path to maintaining and nurturing significant relationships in my journey towards a purposeful and interconnected career.

Cultivating Genuine Connections for Mutual Growth

To form genuine connections within professional networks requires a certain level of artistry. It's about approaching each interaction with authenticity, seeking to understand as much as to be understood, and engaging in active listening. A great way to show this is to make notes before you connect and then take notes during a discussion.

For example, when I ask someone to meet me for coffee or lunch, I like to bring my journal pad and pen and take notes. I don't always take notes, but it's a way to show that I am prepared and interested in what the other person has to say. It can also provide you with information that you can use as a follow-up in a future conversation. If you don't have a notepad, put it in your phone or write it down when you leave. Follow up is the gateway to the next stop on the road of relationship building.

In the realm of intentional networking, the art of forming genuine connections stands as a cornerstone, pivotal to fostering mutual growth and meaningful relationships. To illuminate this vital aspect of networking, let's draw on a personal experience that vividly captures the essence of authentic connection and its impact.

On a hurried morning heading to Austin for a Texas SHRM executive meeting, an unexpected encounter at the airport offered a profound lesson in the power of genuine connections. I was running late and felt anxious about finding a parking spot and making my flight. Upon reaching the last level of the parking garage and finding a spot, I hurried to the elevator. When the elevator door opened, a pilot walked in behind me. He asked, "Where you headed?" I responded, "To Austin," and then he asked, "Are you on the 8am flight?" I said yes, and he answered, "Well, I will be flying you then! My name is Captain Jeff." I smiled and shared my name and that I worked for The Armstrong Company. He then went on to tell me that he had moved with our company and what a great service we provided. It was at that moment I felt relaxed and appreciated the connection he made. But his connection didn't stop there.

When we got to the ticket line, he told me he was going through another line but to say something when I got on the plane, and he would let me check out the cockpit. I thought, "Wow, that would be really cool." When I got on the plane, I mentioned his name and he stepped out and said, "Come on back." It was so awesome! We took pictures and talked about his process of flying. I remember walking back to my seat feeling energized and truly valued.

This story exemplifies the core of forming genuine connections—it's about seizing the moment to turn a routine interaction into an opportunity for mutual growth and understanding. Captain Jeff's approach wasn't about networking in the traditional sense; there was no exchange of business cards or overt professional gain. Instead, it was about creating a moment of genuine connection that enriched both our days.

As we delve into learning how to form such authentic connections, remember that the goal is mutual growth. It's about finding value and meaning in every interaction, understanding that these connections lay the foundation for a network rich in diversity, strength, and collaborative potential.

One powerful strategy for cultivating such connections is to approach conversations with curiosity. Be interested in the stories behind people's career choices, their passions, and their challenges. As leadership expert Simon Sinek suggests, "Start with why." Understand the 'why' behind your new connections and share yours. When people see that you are interested in their motivations and values, they are more likely to engage with you on a deeper level.

Another strategy is to provide value without the immediate expectation of return. This is known as the 100/0 rule. The rule states that when we give 100% of what we have to offer, and expect 0% in return, we will never be disappointed. When we get something back, it will be like a gift. It can also help you sleep better at night. Many times,

> **When we get something back, it will be like a gift.**

we struggle because we are caught up in why someone didn't return something to us. But significance is helping others—not helping others to get something back. Offer your insights, assistance, or support to others freely. This might mean sharing an article you think they'd find interesting, offering feedback on a project they're working on, or introducing them to someone in your network who could help with a problem they're facing.

This approach transforms simple network connections into relationships. It sets the stage for a symbiotic growth where learning, opportunities, and ideas flow freely in both directions. This mutuality is the bedrock upon which networks of significance are built.

Navigating Mentorship: The Compass of Professional Growth

The path to finding mentors—and becoming one—is marked by the pursuit of wisdom and a commitment to pass it on. Acquiring a mentor is similar to having an experienced guide join you on your journey, someone who can help you navigate tricky terrain and point out views you might not have seen. In turn, becoming a mentor allows you to be that guide for someone else, contributing to the cycle of growth.

To find a mentor, start by identifying the qualities you seek in a guiding figure. What expertise do you want to develop? Which career attributes do you admire? Once you have a clear image, engage in communities, both online and offline, where such individuals may be found. Don't be afraid to reach out directly but do so with respect for their time and with clarity about what you're seeking.

Recently, I was watching a roundtable interview with several former NFL quarterbacks including Bret Favre, Tom Brady, and others. During this interview, Tom was sharing a story about a time he worked out with Hall of Fame Quarterback Peyton Manning. Tom talked about Peyton's structured workouts, and how he would line up for certain plays, and when something wasn't working, how he would call out a different play or design a route for his receivers. When Tom returned home, he shared one of the plays with his offensive coordinator, Bill O'Brien, and asked him to add the play or protection during the game. He then went on to call this play and had tremendous success throwing the ball to receiver Rob Gronkowski.

Now this is a great story, but here was the takeaway. During the interview, Tom shared, "Quarterbacks learn from other quarterbacks." This may not be earth-shattering news, but it's BIG. Think about it. Who are you learning from? Do you have an opportunity to go work out with someone successful in your line of work? What plays are they running to start their day? How do they think?

I remember when I started attending different networking events in the human resources and mobility space and seeing a lot of salespeople in the room. I didn't realize it at the time, but I got a front row seat to watch how some of the best showed up to the meeting and how they connected with others. It wasn't about what I could get from the meeting, but what I could learn from those around me. When I realized this, I doubled down on my learning. It's what helped shape my approach to my everyday.

Since then, I have studied great salespeople. I have studied books. I have studied my customers (who are incredible leaders) and others in my community. I have studied leaders in our company and business partners in volunteer organizations. This is where the growth is.

When I was a young manager, I worked for a leader who shared open-book financials with everyone. I always wondered why he did this because of how easy it would be for a competitor to obtain his information. People would fly into Dallas from around the country to learn from him and the strategies he used to operate his company. Today, I realize how others used the 'Tom Brady' approach to learn from this great leader. What's fascinating is they were already great leaders, but they knew that they didn't know everything, and they could learn something.

It's true – the more we give the more we get. But I would also add the more we learn the more we can give—and there is so much to learn on this great journey.

So, who is your quarterback? In other words, who are you learning from? Are you investing time with someone in the workplace? What about outside the workplace? What can you take and put in your playbook to be a better leader, a better salesperson, a better mom/dad, a better volunteer, etc.?

Quarterbacks learn from quarterbacks, and we can all learn from others who have not only achieved success but significance. We just need to have the courage to take that first step and ask. Who around you has achieved success and significance? It may be time to let them know how much you admire them and to connect for a visit. Or maybe it's time to go outside the workplace and get involved in your local association.

> **Quarterbacks learn from quarterbacks, and we can all learn from others who have not only achieved success but significance.**

When asking someone to be your mentor, be specific about why you've chosen them and what you hope to learn. This not only shows that you've done your homework but also that you value what makes their perspective unique. Remember the words of Indra Nooyi, former CEO of PepsiCo: "The distance between number one and number two is always a constant. If you want to improve the organization, you have to improve yourself and the organization gets pulled up with you."

As for becoming a mentor, it's important to recognize that mentorship is a two-way street. It requires listening, patience, and a genuine desire to see another person succeed. Share your knowledge, but also encourage your mentee to find their own path, helping them to develop not only their skills but also the confidence to use them.

Leveraging Platforms for Purposeful Connections

In the digital age, platforms for professional networking are abundant. These tools are not just for job hunting but are rich soils in which to plant the seeds of a significant career.

LinkedIn, for instance, is more than a resume repository; it's a global professional forum. Engage with content relevant to your values and purpose, join groups that align with your professional ethos, and contribute to conversations that matter. Use LinkedIn's publishing platform to share your thoughts and insights, further establishing your voice in the professional community.

Meetup and Eventbrite can be gateways to communities and events that resonate with your career intentions. Search for groups and seminars that focus on the intersection of your industry and social impact. These events can be valuable for meeting like-minded professionals and finding collaboration opportunities.

Don't overlook other social platforms such as Instagram, Facebook, and X (formerly Twitter). We can learn a lot about what moves people from these platforms. There is also the power of informational interviews conducted via Zoom or another video platform. They can be a great way to learn from others and gauge how your skills and values could transition into different roles or industries. It also gives you a way to connect with others and form future relationships.

For example, years ago I was speaking to a group of business leaders in Dallas, Texas via a Zoom meeting. Zoom meetings are challenging when you have lots of people attending. Many times, you are muted, but there is a chat opportunity in most cases to share your voice, to be seen, and ask questions to learn. After the meeting, I received a message on LinkedIn from a young woman who was in transition during her career. She reached out to connect, then followed up with a message to share how much she enjoyed the information that I had shared during the Zoom meeting and how she would like to have a 30-minute follow-up to talk about some of the strategies I had shared. Of course, I agreed.

We later connected over a phone call, and she shared how she was transitioning from the education industry to business and wanted insights. She was genuine and interested. I advised the best way for her to get to where she needed to go without the business experience was to build her network. She could do this the same way she connected with me. I then shared some advice—something that would not only help her build her network quicker but also help her multiply her relationships and land a job in her new industry—and it can help you too. It's what Dale Carnegie, the author of *How to Win Friends & Influence People* always did. Dale Carnegie had the letters "AFAR" embossed on his brief case to remind him when picking up the briefcase to leave a meeting to always "ASK FOR A REFERRAL."

Each time you finish visiting with someone, you should ask, "Can you introduce me to anyone else who would be a good person for me to talk to?" If you were to do this every day for 30 days, you could

Your network is your net worth.

easily have up to 50 new contacts over the course of 60 to 90 days. The key is to find ways to stay connected and continue to look for ways to help the people you have connected with. It's intentional, it's a lot of work, but it's work worthwhile.

Remember, each platform serves as a bridge, connecting you to a broader professional world. Use them wisely, and with intention, to extend your reach and deepen your impact.

I often share a phrase, "Your network is your net worth." What I mean by this is that when I began my career in Dallas, I didn't know anyone. In fact, I didn't get involved with meeting people outside my company until a few years into my career. Once I started networking, I started meeting people. And once I started networking with purpose, I started learning from people, something that has helped me become a better person today. I didn't know where any of this would lead (the 100/0 rule), I just knew that the more I connected, the more purpose it gave me. I have built networks inside my company, outside my company, in my community, among my customers, among parents of my kids' teammates, in toastmasters and speaker groups, and on and on. You can literally network wherever you are. You just need to choose to connect and build. The best part about the journey is that many of these connections turned into business partners, and eventually into lifelong friendships. That's what's so special about networking. It starts with a connection and turns into a friendship. It's quite the journey, but to walk the journey, you must take the step to genuinely connect.

***

As this chapter closes, it's essential to remember that networking with intention isn't a one-off event; it's a continual process that weaves through the fabric of your career. It's about making genuine connections and building relationships that matter, that endure beyond job titles and workplaces. With each connection forged, with each mentorship embraced, and with each tool utilized, you're building a network that not only supports your career but enriches it with purpose and meaning. It is in these connections that the roots of a significant career take hold, allowing you to grow not just upward, but outward, impacting the professional community and beyond.

Drive With Purpose

1. *What are you doing to build your network to ultimately serve others?*

2. *Which connections on your LinkedIn profile do you need to contact to start building relationships? Start searching for resources and share to see what you learn.*

3. *Where can you start using the 100/0 rule in the workplace and in your community?*

4. *Do you ask for referrals using the AFAR approach? Start using this when connecting with others and watch your network multiply.*

5. *What networking groups are you involved in? Once you get connected, find a way to serve, and watch your network transform into friendships.*

CHAPTER 7

Creating Impact Through Leadership

"Before you are a leader, success is all about growing yourself. When you become a leader, success is all about growing others." — Jack Welch

L eadership is the wheel that guides a team's journey towards a meaningful and collective destination. It's not just about steering the car to a specific location, but also about ensuring that the ride is enriching for everyone inside. This chapter explores the vital role leadership plays in shaping careers that are not only successful but also significant, much like a skilled driver who makes the journey as remarkable as the destination itself.

The Beacon of Significance: Leadership's Role

Leadership is the force that transforms a personal vision into a shared reality. It is the capacity to translate vision into action and, more importantly, to inspire others to embark on that mission with you. John Quincy Adams encapsulated this sentiment perfectly when he said, "If your actions inspire others to dream more, learn more, do more and become more, you are a leader." When leadership is rooted in the pursuit of significance, it naturally elevates the mission from individual success to collective impact.

To lead for significance means to recognize that your greatest achievements as a leader are seen in the successes of your team and the positive change your group enacts in the broader community. This kind of leadership is characterized not by personal accolades but by the advancement and growth of others. It's about leaving a legacy of empowerment and service.

> **To lead for significance means to recognize that your greatest achievements as a leader are seen in the successes of your team and the positive change your group enacts in the broader community.**

A leader focused on significance is one who asks not, "How can I stand out?" but "How can we all move forward together?" This shift in perspective is pivotal—it's about harnessing individual strengths for a greater cause, cultivating an environment where innovation and collaboration thrive, and where each member is valued and heard.

Compassionate Navigation: Leading with Empathy and Service

Empathy is the cornerstone of a leadership style that resonates deeply and drives significance. It's the ability to understand and share the feelings of another—a critical skill for leaders who aspire to create a positive impact. Empathy allows leaders to connect with their teams on a personal level, fostering a sense of trust and loyalty.

Strategies for leading with empathy include active listening, where you give full attention to team members, acknowledging their perspectives and feelings. It's also about being present, both physically and emotionally, for your team.

When I think about what it means to actively listen, I am reminded of the time I got to see former President George W. Bush speak at a SHRM conference in New Orleans. As I took my seat, I saw a sign that read, "No recording, no photography, and no taking notes." As an avid note taker, I wasn't sure how I'd survive. I thought about how I was going to have to really focus and listen so that I could write down key takeaways after the session.

As soon as President Bush began to speak, I went into full listening mode—fully present in the moment. My eyes were filled with tears of gratitude and joy as I listened to our former President share his perspective around leadership and the workplace. It was a very moving, uplifting, and emotional experience.

As soon as the session was over, I rushed out to make notes. I even sent a text to others in my group asking for their takeaways so we could combine our notes. I wrote down things like humility, family, and some of the quotes he mentioned. But one of the most important takeaways was his discussion about listening. As former President Bush shared, people can learn a lot about other people when they listen, including listening to how others think. Listening is a skill and when we are in the moment it helps us focus, it engages us, and drives better conversations.

When writing my book, *Life in the Leadership Lane*, I reached out to several top HR leaders and asked them what the most important trait is for developing influence and trust in the workplace. It was unanimous. The importance of listening was on everyone's list. It is a key to building trust in the workplace. It also makes people around us feel more valued when we show that we are listening.

My friend, Chief Human Resources Officer, Mitch Beckman, once shared, "We must listen, relate, understand, and listen more to be an effective leader."

But empathy and listening are just part of the equation. Service-oriented leadership completes this compassionate approach. Leaders who prioritize service act consistently in the best interests of their team and community. They provide resources and support for team members to pursue their passions, especially those that contribute to the greater good. This leadership style is not about commanding from on high but guiding from within, walking the path alongside the team. This requires being intentional in your connections in the workplace.

Taking time to connect in the workplace is a profound way to serve others, as it fosters a culture of support, understanding, and collaboration. In a busy work environment, individuals often focus primarily on their tasks and responsibilities, which can lead to isolation or a sense of disconnection. By actively engaging with people, you create opportunities for meaningful interactions that go beyond mere professional courtesies. These connections can be instrumental in understanding others' challenges, strengths, and perspectives. This deeper understanding not only improves teamwork but also creates an environment where individuals feel valued and supported. When employees feel listened to and understood, it boosts their morale and productivity, ultimately benefiting the entire organization. When clients feel listened to, it builds trust, which can further enhance relationships and business opportunities.

Moreover, connecting with others in the workplace can act as a form of service by providing emotional and professional support. Regular, empathetic interactions can lead to the sharing of knowledge and experiences, offering guidance or mentorship, and even providing a listening ear during stressful times. This kind of support can be especially crucial in creating an inclusive workplace where diversity is respected and different viewpoints are appreciated. Additionally, these connections can lead to identifying and addressing workplace issues more effectively, as employees feel more comfortable sharing their insights and suggestions.

Moreover, connecting with others in the workplace can act as a form of service by providing emotional and professional support.

Taking the time to connect with others at work is not just about building relationships; it's about creating a collaborative, supportive, and empathetic environment that enables everyone to thrive.

107

Combining empathetic listening with service-oriented actions creates a powerful leadership style that can transform a workplace. It's about going beyond mere management to truly leading with heart and purpose, creating a ripple effect of positive change that extends far beyond the office walls.

Uncharted Leadership: Influence Beyond Titles

Leadership is not confined to a title or position. It's about influence, and influence can be wielded from any role within an organization. Those in non-traditional leadership roles often drive significance by championing innovation, advocating for change, and mentoring colleagues informally.

This section explores how individuals without formal authority can exhibit leadership by taking initiative on projects that align with their values, by being vocal about important issues, and by building coalitions to address challenges. Leadership is about action, and every action taken with the intention of contributing positively is an act of leadership.

If you are not in a formal leadership role but wish to serve as a leader in your workplace, here is an action list to guide you in exhibiting leadership qualities and influence:

1. **Identify Opportunities for Initiative**: Look for projects or tasks within your organization that align with your values and

skills. Volunteer for these initiatives, showing your willingness to step up and contribute meaningfully.

2. **Speak Up About Important Issues**: Be vocal and articulate about issues that matter to the organization and its employees. Share your insights and perspectives in meetings and discussions, offering constructive solutions or ideas.

3. **Build Relationships and Coalitions**: Foster connections with colleagues across different departments. Collaborate on projects and create informal coalitions to address common challenges or pursue shared goals.

4. **Demonstrate Consistency and Reliability**: Show up consistently and reliably in your work. Meet deadlines, produce quality work, and be dependable. This builds your credibility and trustworthiness within the organization.

5. **Develop and Share Expertise**: Invest time in expanding your knowledge and skills. Become a go-to resource in your area of expertise and be open to sharing your knowledge with others.

6. **Mentor and Support Colleagues**: Offer guidance and support to your peers. Share your experiences, provide feedback, and be a sounding board for ideas. This informal mentoring can significantly impact team dynamics and performance.

7. **Lead by Example**: Exhibit the qualities and behaviors you value in a leader. Be ethical, responsible, and positive. Your

actions can inspire others and set a standard for leadership within the team.

8. **Promote a Positive Work Culture**: Contribute to a workplace culture that values collaboration, respect, and inclusivity. Encourage open communication and recognize the contributions of others.

9. **Adapt and Embrace Change**: Be open to new ideas and approaches. Adaptability shows your willingness to grow and can position you as a forward-thinking member of the organization.

10. **Reflect and Seek Feedback**: Regularly reflect on your actions and their impact. Seek feedback from peers and supervisors to understand how you can improve and further your influence.

Earning trust becomes your currency, and as you invest that currency wisely, your capacity to lead and influence grows.

By following these steps, you can demonstrate leadership qualities and exert a positive influence in your workplace, regardless of your formal position or title.

When leading without formal authority, it's essential to build credibility through consistency, reliability, and expertise. Earning trust becomes your currency, and as you invest that currency wisely, your capacity to lead and influence grows. Leaders in every capacity can be catalysts for change, driving significance through their actions and initiatives.

Journeys of Significance: Stories of Impactful Leaders

Before concluding this chapter, I'd like to share some stories of leaders who have left indelible marks on their fields by prioritizing significance. These narratives showcase the breadth of leadership styles and the various ways in which leaders can create a lasting impact.

I have been around some of the best leaders in my career. Many I have worked with and continue to work with in our company, while others have led other companies or served as a volunteer leader. As I think about the leadership traits shared above, I think about people like Brad Long, Vice President of Operations at The Armstrong Company, in Dallas, Texas. Brad has served our company for 39 years and counting. He is a great resource for everyone. But what's made Brad so successful has been his consistency. He dresses up for success, and he arrives at the office before 5am each morning to begin planning the day. Brad always knows what is happening and connects with his van operators daily to check in, lending his ear to the constant challenges of moving families locally or across the US. I admire Brad because of his positive attitude. You wouldn't know the challenges he deals with every day unless you were sitting in his chair. He knows that he must adapt to not only keep up with the schedule demand, but also with the changes happening around his moving crews.

Brad is proud of his team, and he shows it by posting scores on his wall, or after hanging up the phone by saying, "Hey, I just got off the phone with our van operator of the year." Every interaction I see with Brad includes mentorship. He is that person that is available, approachable, and willing to share insights. He is ready to listen and teach where needed. Brad leads our operations training meetings and is willing to share his expertise while serving on committees. He is also a listener and willing to consider options when a van operator or customer has a need outside the moving guidelines. Mostly, Brad is a relationship builder. Every time I mention Brad's name in the office, or when on a call to corporate or at industry conferences or events, I always hear the same response: "Brad is the best. Brad's always willing to help us out. When I need something, my first call is to Brad." That's servant leadership—that's leading a career of significance.

I also think about Dr. Sandra Reid, former Chair of the Graduate School of Business MBA Program at Dallas Baptist University. Dr. Reid has been in education for many years, serving students pursuing a master's degree in business marketing. I got a front row seat to Dr. Reid when she became President of DallasHR, and I served as President Elect. Dr. Reid would spend the first ten minutes of every meeting mentoring and sharing her expertise to help volunteer leaders on the board become better leaders, not just as volunteers but in the workplace. She is always teaching and learning. Dr. Reid would also invite experts to come to the school and share their perspective with students in her classes. She listens to everyone, and she is always seeking feedback so she can become more to help her students become more. She is also a relationship builder and always looks for opportunities to help her students drive with purpose. One of the things that impressed me was her project idea to have her students journal during the semester to help them reflect. When the class was over, she would get notes from students about how they appreciated her listening and showing empathy for things outside the classroom.

As a volunteer leader, Rose Ann Garza, Chief Human Resources Officer at Kerbey Lane Café, is another example of leading with empathy. She ends all her meetings with appreciation. No matter if the conversations are fun and engaging or difficult and challenging, she makes sure everyone comes together when the meeting is over to find something they appreciate about another person in the room.

In the healthcare sector, Leah Swanson, Executive Director of the Leukemia and Lymphoma Society of North Texas, leans into her influence as a leader to recruit volunteers to her executive committee to help raise money for people like my niece, Summer Waller. Summer battled leukemia as a child and is thriving today thanks to this organization and leaders like Leah Swanson, who go the extra mile to make a difference. Her contribution to the communities of North Texas was appreciated even more when my oldest son, Adam, was diagnosed with follicular lymphoma, who is also thriving and doing well today.

Not long ago I had Leah as a guest on "Life in the Leadership Lane" podcast episode 153 when she shared the following: "There is always time to be busy, but doing something that really matters—you have to carve out time for that." To watch the full episode, visit https://www.youtube.com/watch?v=aCSxLJY5Z7Y.

***

These stories and strategies throughout the chapter are reminders that leadership is a journey within the broader journey of your career. It's a path that demands courage, empathy, and a steadfast commitment to making a difference. As you cultivate your leadership skills, remember that the true measure of your influence is not in the wealth or power you accumulate but in the positive impact you have on the lives of others and the legacy you leave behind.

Drive With Purpose

1. *Are you listening and leading with empathy in the workplace and in your personal life?*
2. *What leadership qualities above do you exhibit best?*
3. *Who can you seek feedback from to confirm these qualities and help you become a better leader? Send them a note and ask for their perspective.*
4. *Who is someone you admire as a leader in the workplace? Send them a note and share why — they will be impacted greatly, and so will you.*
5. *How can you create more impact from where you are now?*

CHAPTER 8

Overcoming Barriers to Significance

"Most of the important things in the world have been accomplished by people who have kept on trying when there seemed to be no hope at all." — Dale Carnegie

E mbarking on a journey toward a significant career is often met with enthusiasm and a sense of purpose. Yet, as the path unfolds, there are various obstacles that can hinder progress. Recognizing and understanding these barriers is the first step toward navigating through them with grace and resilience.

Identifying the Roadblocks to Significance

Common obstacles on the path to a significant career often stem from internal doubts, external pressures, and the comfort of the status quo. The fear of failure looms large, whispering what-ifs that cloud our judgment and paralyze our actions. Complacency can creep in after initial successes, lulling us into a false sense of contentment that stifles growth. External pressures—from societal expectations to workplace norms—can impose constraints that divert us from our chosen route to significance.

Ambiguity, or the uncertainty of the road ahead, is another significant roadblock in the pursuit of a meaningful career. It manifests as a lack of clear direction or defined goals, making it difficult to chart a confident course toward significance. This uncertainty can arise from rapidly changing industry landscapes, unclear personal aspirations, or even the evolving nature of one's role within an organization.

Another considerable obstacle is the misalignment of personal goals with the needs of the community or organization. This discord can lead to a career that feels unfulfilling or off course, undermining the sense of purpose that fuels a significant career.

As the poet Robert Frost famously wrote, "The best way out is always through."

Each of these barriers is like a mirage on the horizon, challenging our resolve and commitment to our journey's destination. As the poet Robert Frost famously wrote, "The best way out is always through." Acknowledging these roadblocks is crucial in crafting a strategy to navigate around them or push through them.

Let's take a closer look at these roadblocks and how to overcome them.

Fear

Fear, in its many forms, often acts as a significant barrier in the journey from a successful to a significant career. Take, for example, the fear of failure. This fear can paralyze professionals, preventing them from taking on new challenges or stepping outside their comfort zones. A manager might hesitate to propose an innovative but risky project idea, worrying that failure could tarnish their reputation. Such a mindset stifles creativity and growth, keeping one's career trajectory within the safe but limited boundaries of known success.

Another common fear is the fear of rejection, which can deter individuals from seeking new opportunities. This could manifest in a skilled professional being reluctant to apply for a higher position or not voicing unique ideas in meetings, simply because of the apprehension about not being accepted or appreciated. The fear of rejection can lead to missed opportunities for advancement and personal development, keeping one in a state of professional stagnation.

The fear of change, or neophobia, is particularly relevant in today's rapidly evolving work environment. The uncertainty that comes with change can be intimidating. For instance, adapting to new technologies or shifting to different career paths can evoke fear, leading to resistance. This resistance not only hinders individual progress but can also hold back the growth of the entire team or organization.

On a more existential level, the fear of the unknown can be a formidable obstacle. This fear often arises when contemplating significant career shifts, such as transitioning to a different industry or starting a new venture. The lack of certainty about what lies ahead can be overwhelming, leading to inaction and missed chances for achieving a more fulfilling and impactful career.

So how exactly do you overcome fear? Here are some practical tips that I have applied throughout my own career:

1. **Embrace Failure as a Learning Tool**: Understand that failure is an inevitable part of growth and innovation. Instead of fearing failure, view it as an opportunity to learn, adapt, and improve. Each failure brings valuable lessons that can guide future decisions and actions.

2. **Challenge Comfort Zones**: Actively seek out opportunities that push you beyond your comfort zone. This might involve taking on new responsibilities, learning new skills, or even changing your career path. Stepping into unfamiliar territory can be daunting, but it's essential for personal and professional growth.

3. **Cultivate Resilience**: Develop resilience by facing fears head-on and persevering through challenges. Resilience is built over time through experiences of overcoming obstacles and bouncing back from setbacks.

4. **Seek Feedback and Mentorship**: Regularly seek feedback from colleagues, mentors, and supervisors. Constructive criticism can provide insights into areas of improvement and help dispel unfounded fears. A mentor can offer guidance, support, and advice based on their experiences, helping you navigate your fears more effectively.

5. **Set Incremental Goals**: Break down larger goals into smaller, manageable tasks. This approach can make daunting objectives seem more achievable and reduce the fear associated with big leaps. Celebrate each small victory to build confidence.

6. **Practice Mindfulness and Reflection**: Engage in mindfulness practices like meditation, which can help manage stress and anxiety. Reflecting on past successes can also boost confidence and reduce fear.

7. **Visualize Success**: Use visualization techniques to imagine achieving your goals. This mental rehearsal can increase confidence and reduce the fear associated with tackling new challenges.

8. **Educate Yourself**: Knowledge is a powerful tool against fear. Educate yourself about the new roles, skills, or industries you are venturing into. Understanding what to expect can reduce the fear of the unknown.

9. **Build a Support Network**: Surround yourself with supportive colleagues, friends, and family members. A strong support network can provide encouragement and advice when facing fears.

10. **Take Action Despite Fear**: Sometimes, the best way to overcome fear is to take action despite it. Taking even small steps forward can build momentum and diminish the power of fear over time.

Remember, overcoming fear is not about its elimination but about managing and moving forward despite it. Courage doesn't mean the absence of fear but rather the determination to persevere in spite of it.

J. K. Rowling, who knows a thing or two about rebounding from failure, advises, "It is impossible to live without failing at something unless you live so cautiously that you might as well not have lived at all—in which case, you fail by default." As Rowling suggests, the risk of failure is an inherent part of living a full and impactful life. Embracing this risk is often the first step towards moving from a career of mere success to one of true significance.

People often fear what they cannot understand or control, and ambiguity represents a lack of control or predictability.

Ambiguity

Ambiguity refers to a situation or condition of having a lack of clarity, certainty, or definiteness. It is characterized by uncertainty, vagueness, doubt, and the potential for multiple interpretations or outcomes. Ambiguity is not an emotion but rather a quality or state of a scenario, information, or environment.

While different, fear and ambiguity often intersect. Ambiguity can lead to fear, particularly when the uncertainty of a situation makes it difficult to predict outcomes or plan responses. People often fear what they cannot understand or control, and ambiguity represents a lack of control or predictability. However, not all ambiguous situations lead to fear, and not all fears stem from ambiguity. For example, a person may have a clear understanding of a dangerous situation (no ambiguity) but still feel fear due to the perceived threat.

This reminds me of a story author Jesse Itzler shared about "Billy the Bully" in his book *Living with the Monks*. Billy the Bully represented doubt and fear, and Billy would always show up when he was trying to achieve something great like taking on a new role, or writing a book, or trying to get healthy, etc. Billy always made him feel a sense of doubt and fear and made him think things like, "You can't do this" or "You shouldn't do that," and "Nobody cares."

This is a common thread for many people, leaders included. We have all doubted ourselves or felt unsure or unwanted at some point in our career (*I'm raising my hand*).

So, how do we kick "Billy the Bully" out of our head and create momentum in any role?

1. Go back to your **WHY**. When I wrote my first book, I was fortunate to have a friend tell me that you have to know WHY you are doing something. Your why is your anchor. If your why isn't big enough, you'll quit. Your why creates clarity around your values, which can push you through tough times.

2. Stay in pursuit of your **GOALS**. What are your professional goals? Are you in alignment? If you don't know where you are going, who knows where you'll end up. Goals can serve as a compass that gets you to your ultimate destination.

3. Focus on **SERVING** others. When I speak to big groups, I used to get nervous because I would think about how people might view me or disagree with what I had to say. Thinking only of myself, I created a lot of unnecessary doubt and uncertainty. When I turned the focus on serving others, the uncertainty and unsured-ness went away. Yes, I still get nervous, which helps create energy. But now I remind myself that some of the things I am going to share will help others through my experiences, and the doubt goes away. Turn everything away from you and onto serving others with your experiences and how it can help them. This will help to create great clarity and confidence.

4. Be **INTERESTED**. I once heard a story about a company that had a president that was retiring and the company had hired a new president. There was a lady who had worked for both presidents at one point in her career. When people found out, they asked her about the difference in the incoming and outgoing leaders. She said, "The outgoing president was an interesting man, but the incoming president was more interested." Focus on listening and being interested.

5. Be **MISSION DRIVEN**. Many times, when we get in an organization, we get overwhelmed by many projects. The more projects the more people, the more people the more stress, etc. The key to success is to keep perspective and focus on the mission of the organization. Talk to other department leaders

and find out how you can help them achieve success. Make sure it's in alignment with company goals and you will be able to stay on track, even during challenging times.

Former singer/songwriter Charlie Daniels shared a piece of advice during an interview on Dan Rather's *The Big Interview* TV show that resonates profoundly in the context of navigating career ambiguity. When asked, "What advice would you give to others coming up behind you in the business?" he replied, "Don't ever look at the empty seats." This advice is particularly pertinent when facing uncertainties and unclear paths in one's career.

Focusing on the 'empty seats,' or the unknown and uncertain aspects of our professional journey, can be a major distraction. It's easy to get caught up in worries about what hasn't happened, who isn't supporting us, or the outcomes we can't predict. Instead, it's more fruitful to concentrate on the present, the known factors, and the people who are engaged and supportive. By doing so, we can give our best to the tasks at hand and navigate through uncertain terrains more confidently.

In the realm of leadership, this means getting 'back on track' and soaring even when the path isn't clear. Reflecting on this advice, leaders should revisit their core motivations, assess their progress towards goals, and consider how to be fully present and effective in their roles, despite not having all the answers. By focusing on what is within their control and influence, leaders can build momentum and purpose, even in the face of ambiguity.

Navigating through ambiguity, after all, requires a blend of flexibility, resilience, and a willingness to explore uncharted territories. It's about embracing the unknown as part of the journey, understanding that sometimes the path to significance involves learning to drive in the fog, using every bit of knowledge and intuition to move forward, even when the destination isn't entirely visible. Overcoming this challenge means cultivating the ability to adapt and make decisive choices amidst uncertainty, turning ambiguity into an opportunity for innovation and personal growth.

Complacency

In the journey of transforming a career from success to significance, one of the most critical challenges we face is overcoming complacency. Complacency, the comfort in routine and the familiar, often acts as a silent barrier to growth and innovation. It's a subtle yet powerful force that can keep us anchored in the past, hindering our ability to adapt and thrive in an ever-evolving professional landscape.

To illustrate this concept and explore ways to combat it, let's delve into a powerful metaphor from Spencer Johnson's renowned book, *Who Moved My Cheese?*. This story not only highlights the pitfalls of complacency but also provides insightful guidance on embracing change.

In the story, two mice, used to finding cheese in the same spot in their maze every day, are faced with a dilemma when their cheese suddenly disappears. One mouse, Hem, decides to wait for the cheese to return, embodying a complacent attitude. In contrast, his friend chooses to venture into the maze in search of new cheese, representing a proactive approach to change. The following dialogue between them is quite revealing:

> "As Hem saw his friend getting into his running gear, he said "You're not really going out into the maze again, are you? Why don't you wait here with me until they put the cheese back?"

> "Because you just don't get it," Hem said. "I didn't want to see it either, but now I realize they're never going to put yesterday's cheese back. It's time to find New Cheese.""

This scenario is a classic illustration of how complacency can hinder growth. Hem's reluctance to leave his comfort zone and explore new possibilities is a common trap many fall into in their careers. We often resist change, preferring the familiarity of our current situation, even when it no longer serves us.

In my first book, *Find Your Lane*, I discuss strategies to find your purpose in the workplace. A key part of this journey is recognizing when complacency has set in. Complacency often manifests as a reluctance to embrace necessary changes, whether in mindset, skill development, or adapting to new industry trends like AI and organizational restructuring.

Complacency can be deceptive, making us feel safe and comfortable while opportunities for growth and improvement pass us by. It's not just about making changes; it's about understanding why these changes are essential for moving from success to significance.

Consider the following story: There was a man watching a boy fishing. He was excited because the boy was catching fish after fish, reeling them in and releasing them. They were all small and the man knew the boy was trying for a big one. Later the boy's reel got tight; he knew he had a whopper of a fish on the line. He struggled reeling it in but was finally able to do it. When he pulled the fish out of the water, the man's eyes got big as he saw how huge the fish was. The boy then took the fish off the hook, looked at it for a minute, then tossed it back into the water. In disbelief, the man ran down to the boy and asked him, "Why didn't you keep that fish—it must have been at least 14" long!" The boy looked at him and said, "Yeah, but I only have a 9" frying pan."

Can you relate to that? Many times, we are looking for something to fit just right. Like the boy, we often limit ourselves based on our current capabilities or resources, failing to see the bigger picture. This mindset of sticking to what we know, or what we think we can handle, is a clear sign of complacency.

To break free from this mindset, we need to think creatively and be willing to expand our 'frying pan.' This could mean acquiring new skills, changing our approach, or even shifting our goals to accommodate greater opportunities.

My podcast interview with Hall of Fame football coach, Bob Stoops, exemplifies the importance of overcoming complacency. He discussed a pivotal moment when he changed his team's practice approach, a decision met with initial resistance but ultimately leading to a significant victory. This story highlights that even when we are comfortable with our current methods, there is value in exploring new strategies.

The journey from complacency to proactive change is not just about altering our actions; it's about expanding our mindset.

The journey from complacency to proactive change is not just about altering our actions; it's about expanding our mindset. It involves recognizing that sticking to the familiar might be holding us back and that seeking new 'cheese'— new experiences, challenges, and opportunities—is essential for continual growth and achieving significance in our careers.

While it's easy to become complacent in familiar routines, true growth and significance lie in our willingness to seek out new opportunities and challenges. It's about changing our plan or 'pan' to make room for bigger and better possibilities.

To overcome complacency, ignite the passion for continuous growth. Set progressively challenging goals that require you to stretch beyond your comfort zone. Adopt a mindset of lifelong learning and remember the words of Nelson Mandela: "I never lose. I either win or learn." This perspective turns every experience into an opportunity for growth, keeping the flame of progress alive.

External Pressures

External pressures play a significant role in shaping the trajectory of one's career, and they can often impede the transition from success to significance. One of the most common forms of external pressure is societal expectations. These expectations can manifest as predefined notions of what a successful career should look like, often emphasizing financial gain, prestige, or certain titles over personal fulfillment and impact. For instance, a professional might feel compelled to pursue a high-paying corporate job that is esteemed by society, even if their true passion lies in a less traditional or less lucrative field. This societal blueprint for success can steer individuals away from careers that might be more meaningful to them personally and to the community at large.

In the workplace, external pressures can come from organizational culture and leadership. Companies often have their own definitions of success, which may focus on short-term achievements, profits, or competition. This environment can discourage employees from taking risks or pursuing innovative ideas that could lead to significant long-term impact. For example, an employee might have an idea for a new process that could improve efficiency or employee well-being, but they might not pursue it due to a culture that prioritizes immediate results over innovative, long-term solutions. Additionally, peer pressure and the desire to conform with colleagues can lead to a 'groupthink' mentality, stifling individual creativity and the pursuit of meaningful, purpose-driven work.

Moreover, external pressures are not just limited to the professional sphere. Personal responsibilities, such as family commitments or financial obligations, can also impact career choices. Balancing these responsibilities while striving for a significant career can be challenging, especially when significant career paths might require additional time, education, or resources. These pressures can create a conflict between achieving personal success and pursuing a career that is truly significant and aligned with one's values and aspirations. Overcoming these external pressures requires a clear understanding of one's own values and goals, as well as the courage to prioritize them in the face of societal, organizational, and personal expectations.

External pressures require a deft balance of adaptability and firmness. Stay true to your values and purpose while being open to the perspectives of others. When workplace norms or societal expectations seem at odds with your path to significance, engage in open and honest communication to seek common ground or to advocate for change.

In navigating through these barriers, it is vital to maintain clarity about your purpose. Your career's significance is not defined by titles or accolades but by the impact and value you bring to the lives of others. By remaining steadfast in your commitment to this cause, you can navigate through the fog of fear, doubt, and pressure that may surround you.

Balancing Self with Service: Aligning Personal and Communal Aspirations

Striking a balance between personal needs and the desire to contribute meaningfully to others is akin to finding the perfect cruising speed on a long drive—it requires constant adjustments and keen awareness of the conditions around you. Personal needs—including health, family commitments, and financial stability—are the fuel that keeps your engine running. Ignoring them can lead to burnout, resentment, or a career that's running on empty.

One strategy is to set clear boundaries and priorities. Understand that saying 'no' to certain demands means saying 'yes' to others that are more aligned with your values and purpose. Allocate time for self-care, knowing that a well-rested and healthy individual is more effective and impactful.

> **Understand that saying 'no' to certain demands means saying 'yes' to others that are more aligned with your values and purpose.**

Philanthropist and entrepreneur Warren Buffet once said, "The difference between successful people and really successful people is that really successful people say no to almost everything." This can be especially true when striving for a career of significance.

Equally important is ensuring that your career efforts have tangible benefits for others. This balance is not a zero-sum game; personal and communal goals can, and often do, synergize. For example, enhancing your skills can increase your capacity to contribute, and volunteering can expand your network and perspectives, feeding back into your personal growth.

It's also important to remember that there is a season for everything.

I recently interviewed Chief Human Resources Officer, Misti Davis, on *Life in the Leadership Lane* episode 175 about leadership, and we discussed the importance of physical activity. During the conversation, Misti shared that she had recently suffered a back injury and it set her back and limited her while recovering. As she shared this, I mentioned there is a season for everything and there are times when we need to pause or say no while we take care of ourselves or others during different seasons of our life.

For example, if you are a young mom, maybe you hold off on volunteering, or if you are in between jobs and taking care of family members, maybe you minimize networking or look for a different approach. We need to give ourselves grace in every situation.

Significance isn't about doing everything all at once. Giving where you can and when you can is significant enough.

When the Path Diverges: A Troubleshooting Guide

Before concluding this chapter, I think it's important to talk about setbacks—those points in life when things don't quite turn out as planned. The journey to career significance is often marked by moments of both triumph and disappointment. These experiences, especially the setbacks, can serve as powerful catalysts for growth and redirection. My own journey provides a vivid illustration of this dynamic.

In 1989, I found myself in the throes of competition, bowling for a chance to qualify for the PBA US Open. The pinnacle moment came when I rolled a perfect 300 game in the final qualifying round, propelling me into the top five finalists. The energy was palpable as I struck 12 consecutive strikes. However, this high was short-lived as I was eliminated during the match play finals. But what seemed like a shattered dream turned into an unexpected opportunity when a last-minute spot opened for me to compete in the US Open, a tournament I had aspired to since childhood.

After 24 games of grueling qualifying rounds, I faced a harsh reality. Finishing near the bottom of the pack, I grappled with the crushing feeling of disappointment and the looming thought that my professional bowling career would *never* materialize. Looking back, though, this unfulfilled dream was the best thing that *never* happened to me, a blessing in disguise. It was a pivotal point that redirected my career path, leading me to a calling that I could never have envisioned at the time.

This story serves as a reminder that in business and personal life, we often fixate on specific goals or achievements. We believe that reaching these milestones is crucial for our success. However, when things don't go as planned, it can feel like a significant setback or even a failure. Yet, these moments of unfulfilled dreams or apparent failures are often 'set-ups' that propel us towards our true calling. They are the hidden blessings that guide us to where we need to be, though we may not realize their significance at the moment.

As we navigate through our professional journeys, encountering roadblocks and unfulfilled dreams can often lead us to question our path and abilities. Yet, it's essential to recognize that these moments are not just obstacles but valuable learning experiences that can reshape our perspective and approach. The key lies in how we respond to these challenges. By adopting a mindset geared towards growth and resilience, we can turn these apparent setbacks into powerful catalysts for personal and professional development. Here are some suggestions for transforming career barriers into mile markers towards a more meaningful and impactful career path:

1. **Reframe Setbacks as Opportunities**: Learn to view setbacks not as the end of the road but as detours guiding you toward new paths. Each disappointment can be a steppingstone to something greater.

2. **Stay Open to New Possibilities**: Don't cling so tightly to one dream or goal that you miss other opportunities. Be flexible

and open to exploring new avenues that may lead to unexpected but fulfilling career paths.

3. **Reflect and Reassess**: Use moments of defeat to reflect on your journey. Ask yourself what you can learn from these experiences and how they can inform your future decisions.

4. **Cultivate Resilience**: Build resilience by embracing challenges and learning from them. Resilience is key to navigating the ups and downs of a career and emerging stronger from each setback.

5. **Trust the Journey**: Have faith that even if things don't go as planned, you are being led to where you need to be. Embrace the journey with its uncertainties and believe in the unfolding of your career narrative.

By embracing these principles, we can transform our unfulfilled dreams and apparent failures into powerful catalysts for personal and professional growth, guiding us toward a career that is not just successful but truly significant.

***

As we conclude this chapter, take heart in knowing that barriers and detours are an integral part of the landscape when pursuing a career of significance. They test our resolve and commitment but also lead to growth and clarity. With each obstacle overcome, you build not only a more resilient and adaptable career but also a story of perseverance that can inspire others to embark on their own paths of significance.

Drive With Purpose

1. *What roadblocks or barriers are you facing in your career that are holding you back? Fear of rejection? Fear of change or the unknown?*

2. *What can you choose from the list above to help with overcoming fear to move ahead or what would you add that has helped you move past it?*

3. *Do you ever feel like you are stuck with ambiguity, complacency, or alignment? What takeaways from this chapter will help you reset and start driving with purpose?*

4. *What is something that never happened to you in your life that you are now grateful for? Share it with a friend.*

CHAPTER 9

Measuring Your Significance

"The measure of life is not its duration, but its donation." — Peter Marshall

The journey towards a career of significance is not a pursuit for the faint-hearted. It's a dedicated path where the mile markers are often the lives touched and the positive changes enacted rather than the accolades collected. Measuring significance, therefore, requires a set of criteria that reflects the depth and breadth of your impact.

Embarking on this path calls for a deep commitment to personal values and a relentless focus on the collective good. It's about seeking opportunities to make a difference, not just in your immediate surroundings but in the broader community. The true measure of significance often lies in the unseen efforts – the mentorship provided to a colleague, the creative solution that streamlines a process, or the supportive role played in a team's success. These contributions, while they may not always garner public recognition, are the building blocks of a meaningful career.

Furthermore, a career of significance is marked by a continuous journey of learning and growth. It involves adapting to new challenges, expanding your skill set, and staying open to new perspectives. This growth isn't just for personal gain; it's about harnessing these new abilities to better serve others. Whether it's by leading a team through a difficult project, offering guidance to newcomers, or volunteering skills for a community cause, the goal is to use your talents and knowledge to create a ripple effect of positive change. In this way, a career of significance transcends the individual, becoming a conduit for broader societal progress.

The Depth of Your Impact: Criteria for Measuring Actions

The evaluation of your career's significance begins by examining the ripples of your actions. Unlike the traditional metrics of success, such as job titles or salaries, significance is measured by the quality of influence and the capacity for positive change. Here are a few ways to gauge significance:

1. **Depth of Influence:** To gauge the depth of your influence, assess the transformations that have occurred because of your work. How have your actions and decisions fostered growth in others? A good starting point is the feedback from peers, mentors, and those you lead or serve. Their testimonials can

often give you a clear picture of how deeply your efforts are felt.

2. **Breadth of Impact:** The breadth of your impact can be evaluated by the scope of change you've inspired. This can be as localized as improvements within your team or as expansive as contributions to your industry or community. Consider the initiatives you've led, the projects you've contributed to, and the policies you've helped shape.

3. **Sustainability of Contributions:** The longevity of your contributions is another crucial measure. Have your actions led to sustainable improvements? Look at the projects and people you've influenced—are they continuing to grow and thrive even after your direct involvement has ended?

4. **Alignment with Core Values:** Finally, how well do your career actions align with your personal values? As Tony Robbins, the renowned life coach, says, "Success without fulfillment is the ultimate failure." Ensure that your actions not only lead to external impact but also resonate with your inner principles and beliefs.

Feedback is essential for measuring career alignment and contributions, whether coming from your boss, a colleague, or a business partner. It's one of the gauges that helps us understand our depth of influence and impact. When we do things for recognition, we are often disappointed. But we do like to hear about our impact or if we are moving in the right direction. Feedback fuels us to keep going.

When I have the opportunity, I will share testimonials on LinkedIn's platform, or after listening to a podcast or reading a book. I do this because I want people to be encouraged to keep driving with purpose, to continue providing impact. If it helped me, I am sure it would help others. I also know what it's like to receive a note of encouragement. Every time I receive feedback, or a note of encouragement, I think about how it validates who I want to be in my career, and it helps me accelerate ahead. It inspires me to drive with purpose.

Non-Scale Victories

My daughter, Allison, hosts a podcast called *Scaling Back and Gaining Your Best Life*. It's an inspiring podcast about people sharing their weight-loss journeys. All her guests have some of the most amazing stories about their successes and struggles, their mindset before, during, and after the process, and what helped them get back up to start living their best life again. The podcast begins with the guest's journey of transformation to inspire others who are in need of support.

However, the most inspiring part of the show is toward the end when Allison asks her guests, "What is your non-scale victory?" This is all about the joy of the journey, instead of the weight-loss number. It's about the other things that have brought them joy by accomplishing their goal. The responses are heartfelt and inspirational. Examples of the non-scale victories are how good it feels to go to the store to try on clothes and no longer need extenders for airline seats.

Listening to my daughter's podcast got me to thinking about how the question can be applied to our career goals. When we achieve goals, there's always something else we gain besides the achievement itself. Oftentimes we get so focused on achieving the goal we forget about the ripple effects of the achievement. Keeping our 'why' in mind can help anchor us in the joys of the journey.

Here are a few of my non-scale victories as I reflect on my journey as a business leader:

- Goal: Passing a Certification

  Non-scale Victory: It gave me more confidence as a business leader and equipped me to have bigger conversations with others in my field.

- Goal: Writing a Book

  Non-scale Victory: Created a way to share personal stories and lessons learned to help others and further connect with my passion and purpose.

Here are some other examples of how sales, operations, and HR goals can translate into non-scale victories:

- Goal: Increase sales

  Non-scale Victory: Help more people solve problems.

- Goal: Recruiting / Retention

  Non-scale Victory: Create a better place to work.

- Goal: Improve quality and safety scores

  Non-scale Victory: Provide a better customer experience for everyone.

Applying the concept of non-scale victories is important when it comes to measuring significance in your career, as it involves recognizing and valuing achievements that aren't necessarily quantifiable or traditional markers of success, similar to how Allison's podcast guests focus on the joys and personal triumphs beyond just weight-loss numbers. By focusing on non-scale victories, you can find deeper satisfaction and motivation in your career, recognizing that success is multi-faceted and not solely defined by traditional metrics like position, salary, or awards.

By focusing on non-scale victories, you can find deeper satisfaction and motivation in your career, recognizing that success is multi-faceted and not solely defined by traditional metrics like position, salary, or awards.

Applying the concept of non-scale victories to the idea of achieving significance in your career, with a focus on doing more for others rather than personal achievements, involves redefining success in terms of positive impacts on colleagues, the community, and the broader industry. Here are some ways to integrate this perspective:

142

1. **Mentorship and Support**: Providing guidance and support to colleagues, especially those newer to the field, is a non-scale victory. This can include mentoring, sharing knowledge, or being a supportive team player. The success here is measured by the growth and development of others.

2. **Creating a Positive Work Environment**: Contributing to a work culture that is inclusive, supportive, and fosters collaboration is a significant non-scale victory. This is about making the workplace a better environment for everyone, not just oneself.

3. **Community Engagement and Social Responsibility**: Involvement in initiatives that benefit the community or advocate for social causes related to your industry is a profound way to measure significance. This can be through volunteering, leading CSR initiatives, or working on projects that have a societal impact.

4. **Empowering Others to Succeed**: Helping others achieve their goals, whether through direct support, providing resources, or creating opportunities for growth, is a key non-scale victory. The focus here is on the success and advancement of others.

5. **Sharing Successes and Credits**: Recognizing and celebrating the achievements of team members and colleagues, and sharing credit for successes, reflects a commitment to collective achievements over personal accolades.

6. **Contributing to Industry Advancements**: Participating in professional communities, contributing to industry knowledge through research, publications, or speaking engagements, with the aim of advancing the field for everyone, rather than just personal recognition.

7. **Building Networks for Collaboration**: Establishing networks that facilitate collaboration and collective problem-solving within and beyond your organization. This expands the impact of your work to a broader community.

8. **Acting as a Role Model for Ethical Practices**: Upholding and promoting ethical practices in your field, advocating for fairness, and setting a positive example in professional conduct.

9. **Listening and Responding to Feedback**: Actively listening to the needs and feedback of colleagues and stakeholders, and taking actions that benefit the collective good, rather than solely personal interests.

This approach to success captures the essence of a fulfilling career journey, where the value lies not only in the destination or goals attained but in the enriching experiences, relationships fostered, and the positive changes we catalyze in the process. It's more than the goal—it's the journey, marked by the profound and often intangible ways we contribute to the well-being and advancement of those around us.

Navigating the Path: Setting Goals for Significance

Transitioning from a focus on traditional success to one of significance requires a recalibration of goal setting. The goals that pave the road to significance are not concerned with personal gain but rather with the enrichment of others and the world around us.

1. **Establishing Purpose-Driven Goals:** When setting goals for significance, start with 'why'. Simon Sinek, an influential thought leader on organizational leadership, implores us to start with why we do what we do. This introspection will guide you to establish goals rooted in your purpose, ones that aim for a higher contribution.

2. **SMART for Significance:** Adapt the SMART goals frame-work to include significance. Your goals should be Specific, Measurable, Achievable, Relevant to your values, and Timely, with a clear deadline. But also ensure that they are Generous, in that they contribute to others, and Sustainable, meaning they create lasting value.

3. **Prioritizing Impact Over Achievement:** Prioritize goals that emphasize impact. Instead of aiming for a certain position, aim to mentor a number of colleagues. Rather than focusing on a salary target, set a goal to fundraise a specific amount for a cause you're passionate about. It's about shifting the focus from personal accolades to communal benefits.

4. **Creating a Significance Map:** Visualize your goals for significance through a Significance Map, a tool that lays out the intended impacts of your goals across different spheres: personal, professional, community, and beyond. This map should connect your daily activities to the larger vision you have for your life's work.

The Mirror of Reflection

The pursuit of significance is not a linear process; it's cyclical and requires frequent reflection. Reflection allows you to hold a mirror up to your actions and their outcomes, giving you a clear image of where you are in relation to where you aim to be. It's a process that provides insight into what's working, what's not, and what adjustments are needed to deepen your impact.

Consider the practice of reflection as vital maintenance on your vehicle of purpose. Just as a car needs regular checks to ensure it's running smoothly, your career requires routine introspection to maintain its trajectory toward significance.

1. **Scheduled Reflections:** Implement a regular schedule for reflection—be it weekly, monthly, or quarterly. Use this time to ask yourself critical questions: Are my actions still aligned with my values? What impact have I made? What can I learn from what didn't go as planned?

2. **Adaptive Mindset:** An adaptive mindset is crucial. As John Maxwell puts it, "Change is inevitable. Growth is optional." Embrace the inevitability of change and choose to grow from it. Be willing to pivot and evolve your approach based on what your reflections reveal to you.

3. **Feedback Loops:** Create feedback loops with peers, mentors, and those impacted by your work. Their insights can be invaluable in the reflection process, providing external perspectives that can reveal facets of your impact you may not see.

Several years ago, I asked my brother-in-law, Earl Reynolds, if I could interview him for my leadership blog. He was serving in the role of CEO, and I thought it would be great to share perspective for others to learn from him. During the interview, I asked if he had a saying or mantra, and he responded with the following: "I have two mantras that I live by that sum up my core values of doing the right thing and investing in people. I conduct my life and coach my team to ask themselves every day if what they did each day could pass the 'mirror test.' In other words, did they display integrity with their approach to business, people and decision making? In addition, you will routinely hear me say, "It is always about the people." As I challenge my team to live by these [values], I am also reminded to continue to stay true to my values."

What a great measuring stick for all of us to 'look in the mirror' and drive our days with purpose.

Mapping Progress: Tools for Tracking the Significance Journey
As you navigate through your career, having the right tools to track your progress toward significance is as essential as having a map on a long journey. These tools not only help chart your course but also provide motivation and a tangible record of the impact you're creating. Here are a few that I use:

1. **Impact Journals:** Keep an impact journal where you record the outcomes of your actions. Note the moments when you felt you made a real difference, the feedback you received, and the lessons you learned.

2. **Goal Trackers:** Utilize digital tools and apps designed for goal tracking to keep tabs on your progress toward your significant goals. These tools can provide visual progress bars and reminders to keep you focused and on track.

3. **Personal Dashboards:** Create a personal dashboard that displays your key metrics for significance. This might include the number of people mentored, funds raised for causes, or hours dedicated to volunteer work.

4. **Annual Reviews:** Conduct an annual review where you evaluate your career's significance over the past year. Look at the goals you set, the actions you took, and the impact those

actions had. Use this review to set goals for the coming year, building on your successes and learning from your challenges.

Each year, I spend the last two weeks in December creating my goals for the upcoming year. I write them down and note them in my phone so I can quickly review when needed. I also share them with others closest to me as a feedback loop. I did this off and on for many years but started being more consistent when I got intentional about who I wanted to be. I remember deciding to create a list of goals that I would accomplish within 10 years. I heard someone share this concept about how we can design our career or life by looking into the future and making goals as if you already achieved them. So, when I was in my early 40's, I decided to write down goals achieved as if I were 50. Some of the goals listed included things like:

- I am now celebrating 32 years of marriage as if I were that age.
- I now have 2 children in college and one in high school.
- I am a four-time Presidents Club award winner.
- I exercise 4-5 times a week.
- I am an active board member in my community.
- I am debt-free except for my home.
- I have written a book.

Wait—write a book? Yes. It was something I had wanted to do ever since I started writing blogs and posting on my website www.brucewaller.com. I thought it might be a great way to capture some of my personal stories and life lessons to share with family and friends. When I turned 50, I reviewed the list and realized I had accomplished almost all the items except for writing a book. The following year, I wrote my first book, *Find Your Lane*, and published it the following year. The book has since led me to so many non-scale victories, from connections to conversations, keynote speaking events, and hosting a podcast.

As I reflect, I realized a couple of things during this process. First, life is short—10 years goes by fast! Second, writing down goals gives you a compass to help you get to where you want to go and a direction to drive with purpose in your career and life.

***

In closing, remember that the measure of your significance is not just found in the echoes of your accomplishments but in the silent nods of gratitude from those whose lives you've touched. It's the unspoken respect from colleagues who've watched you work tirelessly for the betterment of others. The journey to significance is unique for each individual, but the underlying principle remains the same: It is about leaving a trail of significance that not only defines your career but also contributes to the well-being of your community and society at large.

Drive With Purpose

1. *How do you gauge your influence or impact in the workplace?*

2. *What is a non-scale victory you have experienced in the workplace?*

3. *From the list above, what concepts help you achieve non-scale victories?*

4. *How do you approach goal setting?*

5. *What process do you use for staying on track?*

CHAPTER 10

The Ripple Effect

"I alone cannot change the world, but I can cast a stone across the waters to create many ripples." — Mother Teresa

T he concept of significance in one's career is not an isolated phenomenon. Like a stone cast into a still pond, the ripples of individual actions can extend far beyond the initial splash, influencing broader change and catalyzing a collective momentum towards improvement and innovation.

Every significant act, no matter how small, carries the potential to affect a larger ecosystem. The pursuit of significance at an individual level can set the stage for widespread transformation, influencing organizational culture, industry standards, and even societal norms. It starts with a belief in the power of one—the power of an individual action to inspire, to provoke thought, and to challenge the status quo.

The Influence of Individual Significance

Margaret Mead's oft-quoted words, "Never doubt that a small group of thoughtful, committed citizens can change the world; indeed, it's the only thing that ever has," underscore the monumental impact of individual and collective actions grounded in a shared sense of purpose. When we act with intention and a commitment to service, we become the fulcrum upon which the lever of change rests.

These actions are like beacons, signaling to us that change is possible and desirable. They challenge us to consider our role in the

A career marked by significance, therefore, is not just a personal badge of honor; it's a call to arms.

fabric of our environment. This can lead to a cultural shift where the new norm becomes one of proactive contribution and communal advancement, rather than passive participation in the status quo.

A career marked by significance, therefore, is not just a personal badge of honor; it's a call to arms. It's an invitation to question, to act, and to pursue meaningful endeavors that benefit not just us but the community at large.

Stories of Influence: Impacting Communities and Industries

The narrative of significance is best told through stories – those of individuals whose efforts have reverberated through communities and industries, creating impacts far exceeding their original scope.

One such story is that of professional football player, Damar Romeyelle Hamlin. During the nationally televised game against the Cincinnati Bengals, Hamlin was shown making a tackle then getting up only to fall back down and collapse on the field. He was motionless and the game stopped as medics attended to Damar. The announcers weren't sure what to do and everyone watching the game was stunned in silence wondering if Damar would get up. He was not responding and eventually taken to the local hospital in Cincinnati as the media kept us updated.

We later learned that Damar had suffered a cardiac arrest during the game and survived through the help of medics and healthcare professionals. Hamlin later confirmed that he had an episode of commotio cordis, an extremely rare condition in which cardiac rhythm is disrupted by a blow to the chest during a specific 40-millisecond span in the heart's electrical cycle. The condition is 97% fatal if not treated within three minutes. He was released from the hospital 9 days later, and eventually returned to the game.

It was chilling to see how things can change in an instant. It was also amazing to see the inspiration he brought from the situation as millions of people came together in prayer, posting love, and making the heart symbol with their hands. He brought a world together with love. However, what many people didn't realize was that Damar had been inspiring people since he was a child.

In 2020, Damar was named captain of the University of Pittsburgh football team. During this time, he started a charity focusing on the development and safety of youth through sports. He set up a GoFundMe campaign for the Chasing Millions (Chasing M's) Foundation toy drive, with a goal to raise $2,500. Following his injury in Cincinnati, the Chasing M's campaign grew from $2,500 to over $8 million. Damar was later selected for the George Halas Award for overcoming adversity and the Pat Tilman Award of Courage.

Damar chose a life of significance well before his medical emergency on the field, and he continues to bring light to those he serves.

Another powerful example is that of U.S. Navy SEAL veterans, Clint Bruce and Stephen Holley, founders of Carry the Load. Originally started as a mission to restore the true meaning of Memorial Day, Bruce and Holley have since expanded their organization to honor more than just our military heroes and more than just the one holiday. Carry The Load works to bring all Americans together to participate in honoring our nation's heroes every day. Since 2011, the organization has raised almost $40 million to elevate awareness, continuum of care, and education for our national heroes and their families. To learn more about Carry the Load, visit https://www.carrytheload.org/.

Adam Lowry, founder of Move for Hunger, has also been instrumental in creating hunger awareness around the world. One of the things about Adam is that he has a unique ability to bring communities together with his passion and mission to help feed those in need. I recently experienced this when Adam asked our North Texas Relocation Professionals to be part of a truck pull. This is an event where teams of 5 to 10 people come together to pull a rope attached to a moving truck weighing over 15,000 lbs. It was a great event watching everyone pull together.

While at the event, I noticed a banner hanging over the registration tent that read, "Did you know nearly 4,057,910 people in Texas will go to bed hungry tonight." It got my attention and helped me to realize this was more than a truck pull event. This was an awareness campaign. That day we raised over $15,000 with the help of the signature sponsor, The Armstrong Company. Adam continues to find ways to create waves of inspiration through shared experiences to support Move for Hunger. On October 12, 2023, Adam and Move for Hunger teamed up with several organizations to line up and knock down like dominos 12,952 cereal boxes on the Detroit Pistons Basketball Court to set a Guiness World Record. Not only did he find a way to get others involved, but he was also part of the groups that donated almost 13,000 boxes of cereal to local food banks in the area. You can see the record here https://moveforhunger.org/blog/guinness-world-records-attempt.

These stories, and countless others like them, illustrate how a single person's commitment to helping others can ignite a flame that burns across entire communities, industries, and, in some cases, the world. They highlight how careers rooted in significance do not merely exist within a silo of individual accomplishment but serve as touchstones for collective inspiration and action.

Cultivating a Culture of Significance in the Workplace

The pursuit of significance within a career often starts as a personal endeavor but it gains true momentum when it permeates the culture of a workplace. Cultivating a culture of significance is akin to gardening; it requires planning, nurturing, and the right conditions to flourish. When an entire organization adopts a mindset oriented towards significance, the collective power of its individuals can bring about transformative change.

> **Cultivating a culture of significance is akin to gardening; it requires planning, nurturing, and the right conditions to flourish.**

In 2023, I got to visit with Rory Seidens, Vice President of Human Resources, on *Life in the Leadership Lane* podcast episode 168. During our conversation, Rory shared something that really resonated with me as a high performer. He shared what makes people stand out in the workplace and as a volunteer in the community are the "little extras." This is what high performers do. They find ways to do something that creates more value. They create content for newsletters or blogs, they raise their hand to speak on panels, they volunteer, they take on stretch assignments, they find ways to motivate and energize others. They invest in time and preparation to do the "little extras" each week.

It's the extra degree that authors Mac Anderson and Sam Parker share in their book *212: The Extra Degree*. The book is about how extraordinary results can begin with one small change and lead to maximum achievement. At 211 degrees, water is hot, but at 212 it boils. And with boiling water comes steam, and steam can power a locomotive.

If we want to go beyond success and have significance in our career, we need to look for ways to do the little extras, as well as recognize those that do the same. The more we do, the wider the reach of the ripple.

Here are some little extras that can go a long way:

- Ask leadership about helping with a project.
- Coordinate a monthly team member lunch for the purpose of learning.
- Write a blog about customer success stories in your work.
- Take pictures at company events and share them with the team.
- Volunteer for a non-profit.
- Get involved in your industry association.
- Write personal notes.
- Start a book club or podcast club to share perspectives.
- Write an article for your business association.
- Offer to speak on a panel or at an association meeting.
- Post stories on social media.
- Offer to be a mentor.
- Share tips for achieving success (and significance) within your company.

Leaders and employees alike can encourage a culture of significance by celebrating actions that contribute to the greater good. This can be integrated into the organization through recognition programs, where acts of service and contribution are highlighted and rewarded. Performance metrics can be redefined to include not only financial outcomes but also social impact and employee growth.

At The Armstrong Company where I work, our Chief Customer Officer, Dave Nelson, shares a weekly *Friday Flash*—an email that communicates what is going on around our operating companies each week. What makes it special is that it includes something around our values. Many times, it's a story about recognizing one of our team members or companies, or a note from a customer, or an inspirational story, but it is always tied to our values, what we refer to as our DNA. It's who we are and how we operate each day.

Another effective approach to encourage a culture of significance is the implementation of corporate social responsibility (CSR) initiatives that align with the organization's mission and values. CSR initiatives serve as a tangible expression of a company's commitment to significance, providing employees with opportunities to engage in meaningful work that extends beyond their day-to-day tasks.

For example, several years ago, I got to see keynote speaker, Blake Mycoskie, CEO and Founder of TOMS shoes, share his story at a conference in Las Vegas, Nevada. It was inspiring as he shared his journey growing the company and how it was built on purpose. At TOMS, their model was to give away one pair of shoes for every pair of shoes they sold to those in need. It was marketed as BOGO –Buy One, Give One. So, if you purchased a pair of TOMS, you were also giving a pair to someone in need. Now, that's a ripple effect—not only does the company feel a sense of purpose, but the customer also feels it too. Today, TOMS has changed their BOGO model, but continues to give a large portion of proceeds to support charitable causes.

One of our DNA elements at The Armstrong Company is "Generosity—Succeed and Share". Each of our offices across the US looks for ways to support this DNA in local markets. Our company in Dallas supports Metrocrest Services. Metrocrest specializes in helping families and seniors who are going through a crisis situation to stabilize their lives for a brighter future from emergency financial assistance to financial coaching and education to a food pantry. Several times a year, our Dallas team comes together to collect donations and take them over to the center for support. You can learn more here: https://metrocrestservices.org/.

Training and development programs can also be designed with a focus on significance. These can include leadership tracks that emphasize empathy, service, and community engagement, or skill-building workshops that teach how to align professional growth with societal contributions. I remember years ago hearing a term called "the law of familiarity." It basically states that information shared by someone within the walls of your organization can sound a lot different than when it comes from someone on the outside or a known subject matter expert. Bringing in a speaker for a morning training or "Lunch n' Learn" program can inspire a group like no other. I have been inspired by so many people because of the companies that brought in speakers to train and develop talent in the workplace.

In a culture that prioritizes significance, employees feel a greater sense of purpose and connection to their work, which often leads to higher levels of engagement, satisfaction, and retention. It becomes a self-perpetuating cycle; as the culture strengthens, so too does the impact each individual can make.

Beyond the Self: Scaling Significance

Scaling significance means expanding the reach of your positive impact beyond your immediate environment. This expansion can take many forms, from mentoring individuals outside of your organization to contributing to industry-wide changes or advocating for societal issues.

One approach is to leverage your expertise by speaking at conferences, writing articles, or participating in panels. By sharing your knowledge and experience, you can influence a broader audience and inspire others to take up the mantle of significance in their careers.

> **By sharing your knowledge and experience, you can influence a broader audience and inspire others to take up the mantle of significance in their careers.**

Partnerships with other organizations or involvement in community projects can also serve as conduits for scaling your impact. Collaborating with nonprofits, educational institutions, or other businesses can amplify the effects of your work, allowing you to reach populations and sectors that might otherwise be beyond your scope.

Moreover, technology and social media provide powerful platforms for spreading messages and rallying support for causes. By harnessing these tools, you can extend your influence far beyond your geographic location, touching lives and shaping narratives on a global scale.

Scaling significance is not about the grandeur of the act but the breadth of the resonance. It's a testament to the idea that when you light a candle, you also cast out the darkness in far corners you may never see.

***

In closing this chapter, we reflect on the understanding that significance is a journey that doesn't end at the borders of our individual careers. It's an ever-widening circle that starts with personal commitment and spreads out to encompass teams, organizations, industries, and ultimately, society itself. The ripple effect of significance is not just a metaphor; it's a real and powerful force for change, one that can rewrite the narratives of industries, uplift communities, and leave a lasting legacy that transcends the work itself.

Drive With Purpose

1. *Do you know anyone who is inspiring change and creating significance? Connect to learn more about their purpose and ask how you can help expand their reach.*

2. *What "little extra" can you do to help cultivate a culture of significance in your workplace? Raise your hand or pick something from the list above and act.*

3. *How can you scale significance to positively impact culture in your workplace?*

4. *What is a goal you can add for significance? Discuss with your team ways to include others.*

CHAPTER 11

Rules of the Road

"You are what you do, not what you say you'll do." — Carl Jung

As we embark on the journey to transform our careers from mere success to deep significance, it becomes increasingly clear that the path is not just paved with achievements and accolades, but also with the personal traits we embody. The essence of a truly impactful career lies not only in what we accomplish but also in who we are while accomplishing it. This chapter delves into the pivotal role of personal traits in sculpting a career that is not just successful in conventional terms but is profoundly meaningful and resonant with our core values.

In this exploration, we will focus on three fundamental traits that serve as the bedrock of a significant career: **ethics**, **integrity**, and **authenticity**. Ethics, the moral principles that guide our decisions and actions, is the compass that ensures we stay true to what is right and just. Integrity, the quality of being honest and having strong moral principles, acts as the foundation of trust and respect in our professional journey. Authenticity, the state of being true to oneself, empowers us to engage with our work and others in a genuine and transparent manner. Together, these traits form the pillars upon which a career of true significance is built.

As we navigate through each section, we will uncover how these traits not only enhance our professional journey but also align our careers with our deepest values and aspirations. This chapter aims to inspire a deeper introspection into how we can integrate these traits into our everyday professional lives, thereby steering our careers toward a path of lasting significance and fulfillment.

Ethics—Guiding Principles for a Meaningful Career

In professional life, ethics are the guiding principles that not only direct our actions but also define our character in the workplace. Ethics, in its simplest form, is a system of moral principles that influences our decisions and behaviors. In the context of a career, it encompasses the standards of honesty, fairness, and integrity that we uphold in our professional interactions and decisions. The importance of ethics in achieving a career of significance cannot be overstated. It serves as the moral compass that navigates us through the complex and often gray areas

Ethics, in its simplest form, is a system of moral principles that influences our decisions and behaviors.

of professional life, ensuring that our success is not just achieved, but deserved and sustainable.

Each year, almost half of US employees report witnessing unethical or illegal conduct in their workplaces. The majority of these events go unreported and unaddressed. The cost of unethical behavior can be staggering. More than half of the ten largest corporate bankruptcies since 1980—think Enron, WorldCom, Lehman Brothers—resulted from unethical business practices.

Why do we get off track? In his book, *Ethics 101*, John Maxwell shares three reasons. First, we do what's most convenient. Second, we do what we need to do to win. And third, we rationalize our choices.

On the topic of winning, we often hear about ethics when it comes to recruiting in sports. Everyone knows that it takes great players to win. It gives us an edge when we have the best players or the best equipment. Many times, people will go above and beyond when the playing field is level to tilt the game their way in an unethical way.

Take Lance Armstrong for example. In 2012, this seven-time Tour De France winner (1999–2005) was stripped of his titles after an investigation revealed that he had been the central figure in a doping conspiracy during the years in which he won his titles.

As for ethics and rationalization, many times it's the gray areas that get us in trouble. Have you ever heard of Tim Donaghy? Tim was a professional referee for the National Basketball Association and his story was recently told in a 2022 Netflix documentary called *Untold: Operation Flagrant Foul*. He was the son of a successful college basketball referee and wanted to follow the profession of his father and take it to the highest level—the NBA. There he was at the top refereeing games with Michael Jordan, Charles Barkley and more. He was living his dream career. But Tim liked to gamble and NBA had a policy that prohibited referees from gambling. So, Tim partnered with a friend named Jack to bet on football and baseball games. Jack placed the bets and they would settle up each week. One day, while playing golf, his friend Jack said "Give me some winners in the NBA tonight." So, Tim looked at the betting lines in the paper and gave him three plays. Jack came back the next day and told Tim they all won. So, Jack started increasing his bets. Tim had inside information about who was refereeing the games, access to trainers of injured players, and more. Tim would share information with his friend that others didn't have access to. Jack continued to place bets and win, and as this went on, his friend taking bets caught on to Jack and decided to double down on his bets and won big! One day, the high-stakes bookie taking bets had a fallout with the group and came to Tim and told him that if he didn't continue to provide picks for him to win, he was going to make a call to the NBA and threatened his family. So, Tim continued. Next thing you know, Tim was out of work and on his way to prison. All because he rationalized his choices.

Ethical decisions and behaviors have a profound impact on long-term career success and personal fulfillment. When we act ethically, we build trust with colleagues, clients, and stakeholders, creating a foundation for lasting professional relationships. Ethical behavior also fosters a positive reputation, opening doors to opportunities that might otherwise be closed. Moreover, there is an intrinsic fulfillment that comes from knowing we have acted rightly, aligning our professional actions with our personal values.

However, the path of ethics is not always straightforward. The professional landscape is riddled with challenges and scenarios that present ethical dilemmas. These dilemmas can range from conflicts of interest to issues of confidentiality, to the pressures of meeting organizational targets that might tempt one to cut corners. Navigating these dilemmas requires not only a strong ethical foundation but also the ability to critically assess situations and consider the broader impact of our actions.

To maintain high ethical standards and make sound ethical decisions, several strategies can be employed:

1. **Continuous Learning and Awareness**: Stay informed about the ethical standards in your industry and any changes to laws and regulations. Understanding the legal and ethical framework of your profession is essential.

2. **Reflection and Consultation**: Take the time to reflect on ethical dilemmas and consult with trusted colleagues or mentors. Seeking multiple perspectives can provide clarity and alternative approaches to complex situations.

3. **Establish Clear Ethical Guidelines**: Develop personal ethical guidelines or principles that you can refer to when faced

with challenging decisions. Having clear standards in place can simplify decision-making processes.

4. **Foster an Ethical Culture**: Advocate for and contribute to a workplace culture that values ethics. Encourage open discussions about ethical practices and lead by example.

I have interviewed some of the most talented business leaders over the past few years. During the third season of my podcast *Life in the Leadership Lane*, I decided to ask questions around the topic of ethics. We learn so much when we ask questions, but we also must remember the advice Erica Austin provided on episode 160, "When we ask, we must listen." Here are some of the perspectives shared by some of the leaders I've interviewed.

During my podcast interview (episode 135) with Chief People Officer, Shonna Andersen, she shared how her organization invests in 360 reviews—evaluations by employees that surround the leader, including subordinates, peers, colleagues, and supervisors. These reviews provide feedback for the leader on how well he or she is performing in the eyes of those around them. They also help to create a conversation about behavior, which in turn cultivates trust. She also shared how building a great culture of ethics in your company starts with including others in the interview process to help make sure you are bringing in the right people who align with your company values.

In episode 141, Human Resources Director, Rosalinda Quiroga, talked about how the word ethics comes from the Greek word "ethos" and how it means "a way of living." She also talked about how sharing stories about ethics and the importance of recognizing employees helps "cultivate" them into the organization. One of the ways her organization does this is by presenting "The Extra Mile" award to employees that go above and beyond.

Chief People Officer, Jeri George, shared on *Life in the Leadership Lane* podcast episode 140 that ethics issues often come up when we have low employee morale, a lack of communication, and when we don't empower our team members. However, we can counter these by offering training when we see areas of struggle. When Jeri leads her training, she uses a motto, "It's not I gotcha, but I'll get you there," to build trust with her employees and open lines of communication for sharing. She concluded with how it takes time to build trust with others.

Upholding ethics in our career is not just about avoiding wrongdoing; it is about actively contributing to a professional environment that is just, fair, and worthy of the trust it is granted.

By integrating these strategies and perspectives into our professional lives, we strengthen our ability to navigate ethical challenges effectively. Upholding ethics in our career is not just about avoiding wrongdoing; it is about actively contributing to a professional environment that is just, fair, and worthy of the trust it is granted. As we progress in our careers, let us remember that the pursuit of significance is underpinned by the steadfast adherence to the ethical principles that define not only what we achieve but who we are as professionals.

Integrity—The Bedrock of Trust and Respect

Early in my career, I was in a leadership training session with our team, including other executives. The trainer provided everyone with a sheet of paper with 50 values written on it and asked us to circle our top 10 values. He then asked everyone to number their top 5 values, starting with the most important value. I numbered my values and put down my pen. The next part was one of the most impactful moments in my career. The trainer asked who had integrity as their number one value.

At the time, I didn't realize the importance of integrity, simply because I wasn't clear on what it really meant. But when the trainer asked who had integrity as their number one value, every single executive sitting in the room raised their hand except for me. So, I immediately wrote a 1 next to the word on my paper and said to myself, "This is important. I need to make sure I understand it and how to apply it to my every day." Here's what I've learned.

Integrity is often referred to as the bedrock of a credible and respected career. It is the quality of being honest and having strong moral principles, which are non-negotiable in the realm of meaningful professional success. Integrity is not just about doing the right thing when everyone is watching, but maintaining those standards even in the absence of onlookers. The significance of integrity in building a career cannot be overstated; it fosters trust and respect, which are essential for sustainable success and a reputation of reliability and honor in one's field.

In the workplace, integrity underpins every interaction and decision, forming the foundation of solid relationships with colleagues, clients, and stakeholders. It is the consistency of actions, values, methods, measures, principles, expectations, and outcomes. When professionals demonstrate integrity, they build trust—a crucial element in effective teamwork, collaboration, and leadership. Clients and stakeholders are more likely to engage with and invest in individuals and organizations that display high levels of integrity, as it assures them of ethical practices and quality services.

Real-life examples abound where integrity has been a pivotal factor in career advancement and success. Consider the story of a mid-level manager who was offered a lucrative deal that, while beneficial in the short term, involved cutting corners in a way that compromised the company's values. By choosing to decline the deal and propose an alternative that adhered to ethical standards, the manager not only protected the company's reputation but also gained the respect and trust of senior leadership. This decision marked a turning point in their career, leading to greater responsibilities and eventual promotion.

Cultivating and upholding integrity in various professional situations can be challenging, particularly in environments where short-term gains and pressures can overshadow ethical considerations.

However, maintaining integrity is essential for long-term career fulfillment and impact. Here are some strategies to cultivate integrity:

1. **Set Personal Standards**: Define what integrity means to you in a professional context and set clear standards for your behavior. Know your values and the ethical lines you are not willing to cross.

2. **Practice Transparency**: Be honest and transparent in your communications and decisions. If you make a mistake, own it and take steps to rectify it.

3. **Seek Ethical Solutions**: In complex situations, strive to find solutions that align with ethical practices and principles. This may involve creative thinking and collaboration with others.

4. **Lead by Example**: Model integrity in your actions. As a leader or team member, your behavior sets the tone for others.

5. **Build a Supportive Network**: Surround yourself with individuals who value and practice integrity. A supportive network can provide guidance and reinforce ethical behaviors.

6. **Stay Informed**: Keep abreast of ethical standards and practices in your industry. Continuous learning helps in making informed decisions that align with integrity.

By embedding integrity into the fabric of our professional lives, we not only build careers that are successful but also deeply respected and meaningful. Integrity is the compass that guides us through the complexities of our professional journey, ensuring that our path to significance is both ethical and sustainable.

Authenticity—Being True to Yourself and Others

Authenticity in the professional sphere refers to the act of being genuine and true to one's own values, beliefs, and personality, regardless of external pressures or expectations. It's about aligning your actions and words with your authentic self and presenting this true self in your professional interactions. In an era where personal branding has become intertwined with professional success,

> **Integrity is the compass that guides us through the complexities of our professional journey, ensuring that our path to significance is both ethical and sustainable.**

authenticity stands out as a vital trait for meaningful and sustainable career development.

The benefits of being authentic in the workplace are manifold. Authenticity helps in building genuine connections with colleagues, clients, and stakeholders. When people sense that you are genuine, they are more likely to trust and engage with you on a deeper level. This trust is crucial for effective collaboration, leadership, and long-term professional relationships. Additionally, authenticity can inspire others in the workplace, encouraging a culture of openness and honesty, which can lead to enhanced creativity and productivity.

However, maintaining authenticity can be challenging, especially in diverse workplace cultures where there may be a perceived need to conform or mask one's true self to fit in or succeed. Navigating professional environments that have distinct cultures, norms, and expectations can often require a delicate balance between adapting and staying true to oneself. For instance, in a highly competitive corporate environment, expressing vulnerability or uncertainty—aspects of one's authentic self—may seem risky.

When I was younger and first promoted to management, I thought I needed to be someone different, and not get too close to my employees. I felt I needed to be more like the leaders I reported to and stay focused on business results. I later learned this is a myth. When we are authentic, we can show up as ourselves every day, we can focus on building relationships with people, we can focus on business goals and objectives, and we can focus on what matters most—no matter who's around us.

To practice authenticity while adapting to professional roles and environments, consider the following tips:

1. **Know Yourself:** Spend time understanding your values, strengths, and areas for growth. Self-awareness is the first step towards being authentic.

2. **Communicate Openly and Honestly:** Share your thoughts and feelings honestly, but also considerately. Authentic

communication does not mean being blunt or insensitive, but rather being honest in a respectful and appropriate manner.

3. **Set Boundaries**: Understand your limits and communicate them clearly. Setting boundaries is an important part of being authentic and can help prevent burnout and resentment.

4. **Seek Alignment**: Look for aspects of your role or organization that align with your values and strengths. Focus on these areas to bring more of your authentic self into your work.

5. **Embrace Vulnerability**: Being vulnerable at times can be a strength. It allows others to see the real you and can foster deeper connections and understanding.

6. **Adapt While Staying True**: Recognize the difference between adapting to a role or environment and losing your sense of self. Adaptation can be about finding ways to fit in without compromising your core values and identity.

Authenticity in your career path doesn't just lead to success; it paves the way for a journey that is both fulfilling and true to yourself.

By cultivating authenticity, you'll not only enhance your own career satisfaction but also contribute to creating a more genuine and supportive workplace. Authenticity in your career path doesn't just lead to success; it paves the way for a journey that is both fulfilling and true to yourself.

Merging Traits with Action

As we reach the end of this exploration into the essential traits for transforming a career from success to significance, it becomes clear that ethics, integrity, and authenticity are not just admirable qualities but critical drivers for a fulfilling professional journey.

Ethics, serving as our moral compass, guides us to make decisions that are not only beneficial but also just and right. Integrity, as the foundation of trust and respect, builds the credibility necessary to foster strong and lasting professional relationships. Authenticity, the courage to be genuine in all our interactions, allows us to connect deeply with others and bring our whole selves to our work. Together, these traits form a powerful triad that can steer any career towards a path of true significance.

But what happens when we falter in these areas, or make mistakes? Understanding that perfection isn't required from the outset, and that improvement is a continuous journey, can be illustrated through a personal experience of mine.

Growing up in Oklahoma with bowling proprietors as parents, I was deeply immersed in the world of bowling. I recall the excitement of scoring 180 while bowling with my mom at the age of 7, which was a proud moment during our parent-child regional tournament. Another significant memory was when my dad installed one of the first automatic scoring systems in the country, revolutionizing how scores were recorded in the game of bowling. However, it was during a practice session with these new scorers that I learned an important lesson. After starting with a split, I found myself alone and decided to reset the score for a better start. So, I lifted the panel and figured out how to restore the score. I pushed the button and the score disappeared. Then I got back up to bowl and made a strike, exactly how I wanted to start the game. Then I got a spare and was on my way. But then my dad came around the corner and said, "Hey, I thought you started off with a split?" Gulp! He had been watching the entire time.

My desire to start over is a sentiment many of us can relate to, whether it's in our day-to-day lives, relationships, careers, or other endeavors. The key takeaway is that we don't always need to start over. We can begin from where we currently stand. Our past actions and decisions reflect who we were at the time, but they don't dictate our future paths.

This idea is echoed by a famous author who, when asked about his favorite book among the 80 he had written, replied, "It's always my next one." This tells me he has learned things since the first book that have helped him write the next book. He can't go back and change his first book because that's who he was when he wrote it. His response highlights the evolution of learning and growing with each new endeavor. We can't change our past works or actions, but we can use them as steppingstones for future growth and improvement.

Just like in bowling, where a split in the first frame doesn't define the game's outcome, in life and careers, our initial missteps are not endpoints. They are opportunities to learn, grow, and strive for better outcomes in our continual journey towards significance.

Have you ever wished you could restore the score in your life or career? As you reflect, keep the following points in mind:

1. **Start where you are.** Improvement and change can begin in your present situation, whether it's in a job, a relationship, learning a new skill, or personal growth. The idea is to take proactive steps towards your goals from wherever you stand today.

2. **Learn from Your Experiences.** Continuous learning and growing from past experiences are key to progress.

3. **Get comfortable with change and challenges.** It's important to be comfortable with failures and challenges, understanding that they are opportunities for growth and trying again.

4. **Embrace significance over success.** Sometimes significant lane changes are required to move beyond just being successful to achieving something truly significant and impactful.

5. **Be intentional in your actions.** Achieving significance requires being intentional in daily life and setting goals. Sharing your intentions and goals can also help you gain perspective.

6. **Be resilient and finish strong.** Don't let initial setbacks hold you back. And don't be afraid to let go of the good to go for

the great! It's not about how you start; it's about how you finish.

Later in life, I once again bowled a split in the first frame. But instead of starting over, I started where I was and went on to bowl 11 strikes in a row, ending with a final score of 278. Though it wasn't a perfect game, I overcame the setback and finished strong.

Life is full of opportunities to do something special. You just need to start where you are. Start connecting with others, start building new relationships, and always ask, "How can I be of help?" It's also important to be okay with failure or things not working out, because you can always try again. With each attempt, you'll grow stronger and closer to achieving something truly significant.

> **Life is full of opportunities to do something special. You just need to start where you are.**

Years ago, I received a call from a customer needing assistance with a relocation. He inquired about scheduling a moving survey to obtain an estimate and mentioned he would be getting two estimates to determine the best fit for his needs. We arranged the survey for the following week. However, a week later, while reviewing my calendar, I realized the survey had disappeared from my schedule, and I had missed the appointment. This realization was stressful; I had let the customer down by not fulfilling my commitment. After pondering whether to ignore it, make up an excuse, or own up to my mistake, I decided to call the customer, admit my error, and offer to reschedule for the next day. To my surprise, he mentioned that the other company's surveyor had also missed their appointment. Thankfully, he gave me another chance. The next day, I conducted the survey and ultimately secured the move. This experience, starting as a failure and turning into a success, underscored the importance of authenticity and transparency, especially in challenging situations.

As you reflect on your own career, consider how ethics, integrity, and authenticity are currently manifested in your professional life. Are your decisions guided by a strong sense of ethics? Do you consistently act with integrity, even when faced with challenging situations? How often do you allow your authentic self to shine through in your work? Reflecting on these questions can reveal areas where you excel and aspects that may need further development. Remember, the journey towards significance is ongoing, and there is always room for growth.

To continuously nurture these traits, commit to regular self-reflection and seek feedback from trusted colleagues or mentors. Stay informed about ethical practices in your field and remain open to learning and adapting. Practice authenticity by consistently aligning your actions with your values, and remember that integrity is built through small, consistent actions over time.

***

In conclusion, merging the traits of ethics, integrity, and authenticity with action is not a one-time task but a continuous process of personal and professional growth. By committing to these principles, you set yourself on a path not just toward career success, but toward a career that is truly significant—one that is rewarding not only in achievements and accolades but also in personal satisfaction and impact. As you move forward in your career, let these traits be your guideposts, steering you towards a journey that is as meaningful as it is successful.

Drive With Purpose

1. *What would you add to the list above to help you maintain high ethical standards and make sound ethical decisions?*
2. *How have you developed trust in the workplace and how do you keep it?*
3. *What are some ways you practice authenticity?*
4. *Instead of "restoring" your career, what can you do to start where you are now?*
5. *How can you stay informed and share the importance of ethics with others?*

CONCLUSION
Your Roadmap to Significance

"Only a life lived for others is a life worthwhile." — Albert Einstein

As we reach the end of our shared exploration, it's time to reflect on the path we've traveled and look ahead to the roads that beckon us forward. Our expedition has not been about climbing the corporate ladder swiftly but about ensuring each rung we ascend elevates others with us. This journey is rich with intention, marked not by the milestones of status but by the markers of impact we leave in the lives of others.

We began with an understanding that true fulfillment in our careers goes beyond the personal accolades and nestles in the legacy we create. The mindset shift toward service, growth, and purpose we've discussed is the foundation upon which a meaningful career is built. It's about seeing our daily work as an opportunity to contribute, to mentor, to innovate, and to change the fabric of our communities for the better.

Your career is not a road traveled alone; it's a shared path where the connections we make, the help we offer, and the alliances we build are what give our professional lives depth and resonance. We've seen that leadership is less about the authority we hold and more about the influence we wield, and that influence is strongest when used in service to a greater good.

Along the path, we will encounter obstacles—fear, ambiguity, complacency, external pressures—but these are not stop signs; they are detours that test our resolve and sharpen our focus. In facing them, we learn, we adapt, and we grow. We've also equipped ourselves with the tools to gauge our progress, to ensure that we remain steadfast and true to our course.

Your Action Plan for Moving Forward

As you embark on this journey of personal and professional growth, consider the following action plan as your guide. These steps are designed to help you align your career with your deepest values and aspirations, ensuring that every step you take is not just towards success, but towards a life of significance and purpose.

1. Conduct a regular purpose audit to keep your career aligned with your values.
2. Cultivate a mindset of growth and service every day.
3. Reassess your career path periodically to ensure it leads to significance.
4. Build and nurture relationships with the intention of mutual growth.

5. Step into leadership roles, formal or informal, with empathy and a vision for change.

6. Embrace and overcome challenges, viewing them as opportunities for growth.

7. Measure your impact through reflective practices and adjust your course as needed.

8. Look for ways to expand your influence beyond yourself, to your community, and beyond.

With your roadmap in hand, I encourage you to stay in pursuit of significance with confidence and resolve. Remember, significance is not a distant summit to be conquered but a horizon that continually expands as you approach.

Serving others, no matter the scale, can have a profound impact. This is exemplified by some of the most inspirational figures in my life: my grandmother, who became a nurse while raising her children alone after losing her husband in the war; my parents, who steadfastly supported my siblings and me through school; my father-in-law, a dedicated U.S. Marine; my mother-in-law, who took on the care of her sisters

Remember, significance is not a distant summit to be conquered but a horizon that continually expands as you approach.

in their time of need; my wife, who balanced a career in education while nurturing our children and later, our grandchildren; my daughter, aiding those facing weight-loss challenges; and my daughter-in-law, contributing to the medical field as a pathologist.

You don't have to undertake grandiose actions for them to hold great significance. You just need to lean into a life of meaning by seeking ways to help others.

Let the final call to action be one that echoes in your heart every morning: Wake up with purpose. Work with intention. Lead with compassion. Network with sincerity. Face challenges with courage. And above all, leave a trail of significance that others may follow. Strive not just for success in the traditional sense but for the profound satisfaction that comes from knowing you've made a difference.

More Than a Cup of Coffee

If you haven't noticed, I love sharing stories. So, here's one last story for the road.

The day was April 5, 2022, and I had just left Carl's Jr. in Duncan, Oklahoma with several biscuits for my family and a cup of coffee. I remember this day very clearly, as it was the day my father-in-law, Dewey, was laid to rest after 85 wonderful years. He used to visit this restaurant regularly and always ordered the same meal, an extra-extra crispy bacon and egg biscuit with a slice of tomato and a cup of coffee. The entire staff knew his name and each time he walked into the restaurant everyone would whisper "Dewey's here," prompting the team to start cooking his order. He was like a celebrity there. When he finished, he would always tip the staff with some change and wave on his way out.

I am very grateful for the way the staff treated Dewey, how they served him and created such a great experience for him—it's what brought him back each day. And it was the reason I visited the restaurant that day to order the "Dewey Special" for my family in honor of him.

While I was there, the staff shared how they knew about Dewey's passing and how sorry they were. They shared how much they enjoyed him coming in each morning and shared stories about him. They were so compassionate, and the moment was very emotional. In fact, I'm getting emotional as I reflect on the story right now. Everyone behind the counter felt a sense of purpose in their job. They knew the work they were doing impacted everyone coming in. They were driving in the lane of *significance*.

Let this story serve as a reminder that your work is your message to the world—let it be one of hope, of help, and of *significance*. With this mindset, go forth with the courage to transform your piece of the world. Let your career be more than a journey—make it a testament to the difference one person can make when they choose to drive with purpose.

Enjoy the journey!

Journeys from Success to Significance

"What counts in life is not the mere fact that we have lived. It is what difference we have made to the lives of others that will determine the significance of the life we lead." — Nelson Mandela

A s I was driving back from Oklahoma with my wife, we were talking about moments of change in our career. She was sharing one of the biggest changes for her was when she decided to take a lateral position as a teacher and move into a director position for childcare services. She asked her supervisor if it would hurt her chances to continue moving toward becoming a principal and administrator, and she was told it would. But my wife knew the direction she wanted to go and served in that position for the remainder of her career. She touched so many lives caring for other people's children and was a gift of influence and significance to many.

Hearing stories of those who have pivoted their careers from mere success to one of significance can be incredibly enlightening and motivating. These narratives offer valuable insights into the transformative journey of redefining one's professional objectives, highlighting the profound fulfillment that comes from aligning work with personal values and the greater good. They serve as powerful reminders that career success isn't solely measured by traditional benchmarks like status or income, but also by the impact we have on others and the legacy we leave behind.

As we absorb the experiences of these trailblazers, we often find ourselves inspired to evaluate our own career paths. Their stories can ignite a desire within us to seek more meaningful and purpose-driven work, encouraging us to think beyond our individual achievements and consider how our professional lives can contribute to a larger narrative of positive change and communal upliftment. In essence, these stories don't just provide inspiration; they challenge us to envision and pursue a career that transcends personal accolades and becomes a vehicle for significant, life-enriching contributions.

In this final illuminating chapter, you'll gain perspective on what it means to transform a career from mere success to significance from people who have done just that. The stories you are about to read are more than mere narratives; they are powerful testaments to the human spirit's capacity for growth, change, and meaningful impact. Each story is a unique journey of an individual who dared to step beyond the conventional measures of success—titles, accolades, and financial gain—to embrace a path marked by deeper purpose, service, and positive influence on others.

These storytellers come from a variety of backgrounds and industries, but they share a common thread: a pivotal moment where career success, as traditionally defined, no longer sufficed. Their aspirations evolved, seeking fulfillment not just in professional achievements but in contributions that resonate and reverberate through the lives of others. From corporate executives who shifted their focus to fostering growth in others, to teachers who found ways to inspire and educate, each narrative unfolds the transformative power of aligning one's work with a broader mission.

As you read these accounts, you'll see that their journeys aren't just about changing career paths but about altering life trajectories. They remind us that a career, no matter how successful, finds its true fulfillment when it transcends personal achievement and becomes a conduit for making a tangible, positive difference in the lives of those around us.

Here are the stories. I hope you draw as much inspiration and wisdom from them as I have. May they help you find the spark to ignite your own shift from success to significance.

> *When did I move my career from success to significance? I remember the day clearly. It was a normal day, busy with lots of meetings and urgent situations. The job always had me going from one thing to another, but it wasn't fun anymore. The work became monotonous, although it was very important to the leaders and the overall success of the company. There wasn't any satisfaction in the work, so I looked for more meaningful work. My goal was to work somewhere that I could create and build. Somewhere that wanted to innovate, welcomed new ideas and encouraged out of the box thinking. I wanted my work to have meaning, to have significance. In*

the end I wanted to impact people's lives and bring the People function into a more forward-thinking organization. I was lucky enough to have found this in my current leader and company. We are creating and transforming an organization at the speed of light, and it is exhilarating. Now that I have seen the shifts in my organization, I'll never think of success in the same light. I'll always shoot for significance.

— Leslie Mensching

———————

As my full-time career begins to wind down toward my next chapter in life, I find that I have so much to reflect upon and be thankful for regarding the choices I made throughout my journey. It was a journey with many unexpected turns but ultimately helped me to purposefully shift from a career of success to significance.

Starting out as a college graduate, I embarked on a career in financial services, despite having a journalism degree. Driven by energy and curiosity, I quickly climbed the corporate ladder, reaching a vice president position that oversaw the entire operational area where I started. At that time, I felt that I had found success in my responsibilities, my title, great compensation, and recognition. Yet, in my early thirties, I felt that something was missing.

At that point in my life, I placed a high priority on what I defined as my "success." For me, success was about that next promotion, the bigger office, a higher title, and of course a higher salary. However, I quickly learned that the satisfaction that came from these so-called successes was short-lived. For with each success came stress, internal politics, burnout, worry, and a lack of fulfillment. I knew that this was not a lifelong trajectory, but I did not know where to go from here.

After multiple job changes, research, and most importantly, self-reflection, I began to focus on what I really wanted to do and what I identified as missing from my career. It was significance—the joy of serving others and impacting lives. This led to a career change to human resources, starting with resigning from my finance job and enrolling in graduate school for human resource management.

After earning my master's degree and a certification in human resources, I embarked on a fulfilling career in the human resources industry. Although it took years to regain my previous salary levels and I never reached the same titles, the work felt significant and satisfying.

Fast forward to today, I have enjoyed a 20+ year career in human resources, contributing in various roles from Policy Advisor to Assistant Director of Human Resources for a Division I college athletics program. Each position allowed me to apply my servant leadership traits, help others, and make a real impact in the lives of countless employees. To me, this was significance in action.

While I may not have the high-level job title, 401K balance, stock options, and all the other perks I once associated with success, I feel blessed with what I've achieved. By embracing significance over comfort, I've experienced incredible growth. Now, as I look toward my next path toward significance, it will involve taking these past experiences and leveraging them through mentoring, coaching, serving, and volunteer leadership to reach even higher levels of significance by giving back to the future generation of human resource professionals and as such, I will be achieving both significance and success.

— Jeff Palkowski

————————

Over the course of nearly eight years, I held the position of Director, HR supporting field and corporate teams and serving as back-up to our services business and manufacturing facility. I achieved notable success, evidenced by two well-deserved promotions. Despite the accomplishments and growth opportunities presented in my current role, a pivotal moment arose when the CHRO approached me with a new opportunity to lead the Talent Acquisition team. Initially, I found myself lacking enthusiasm for this new opportunity, given my comfort and success in my existing role. This new role was vacant, and the challenge presented involved the reconstruction of the team, and the fostering of growth and development within the team. I quickly learned that this role offered more than just another career progression. It presented an avenue for achieving greater significance in my professional endeavors. I'm more fulfilled in this new role as I'm able to add more impact to not only how we attract new talent as a team, but how we value each team member's contributions and build careers.

— Jamie Son

During my undergraduate years, I was working as a legal assistant at a law firm and going to school in Alabama. My HR manager wouldn't let me clock in until 8 am on the dot, and if I was there past 5 pm, he was literally at my desk right at 5:01 making sure I clocked out. I recall a time when we were preparing for trial, and I got to work early to make sure everything was in order, and he wouldn't let me clock in. I had to sit and wait until 8 am. And as we closed the day, even if I had 5 more minutes of work to close something out — I was asked to clock out and come back to it the next morning. From this experience I knew very early on I would work as hard as I needed to move out of an NEX status. I wanted more meaning to my work, career journey and time. I did not want to live by a timeclock. I still keep in touch with this HR manager today — he is a great man. But the experience very much shaped everything I wanted career-wise from that point forward.

— Shelly Mullins

—————

My lane changed when I realized I had a calling vs JOB...one that wasn't a path like others...it was a winding road, it was bad weather at times, often lonely, seemingly full of obstacles / potholes trying to say "I didn't belong...X"". Every single time I cried out to God to release me from this crazy dream that surely was mine & not His...He would send someone to be His messenger, to encourage, to provide, to calm my fears & yes, dry the tears. When I graduated from UNT & began as a faculty member at DBU, for at least the first year I told my VP I just didn't belong here...I had industry mentality & I just did not fit the landscape.

As I became really immersed in the life of academe, I had various administrative roles, but I was also in front of students...especially graduate students. Single Moms. First Generations. Returning to school after decades away because they had feared they couldn't do it men and women. Yes, even the homeless living out of their car. Determined, persistent, incredibly sacrificial & their eyes firmly planted on a God-given goal to complete a master's degree in business as fast as possible really. My deep belief is He doesn't bring "you here to leave you here" wherever "here" is. I deeply wanted them to know what I knew...if I could do it, THEY COULD DO IT. Laid on my heart was to journal with students...I had to connect to their heart & mine to theirs. You see, I wanted to be good enough. And I already knew they were. It was in really my first semester of heart connections in my first year, that was my pivotal jump to significance. How did I know? I knew because one after another told me in their journals, visits with me at Graduation, as Alumni, etc., that I had helped them get to where they never really thought they would get, they believed they could not have done it without me & my love for them...His love shining through me, you see. I realized one pivotal night that all had been sent & so had I. And at that point, absolutely then, I knew I no longer had a job, I had connection directly to impact, yes, significance. For me, my life changed forever with that very first student & His words to me to keep going, I was, indeed, sent to do Kingdom work.

— Dr. Sandra Reid

———————

The time I shifted was this year when I decided to go back and get my Masters. The thought is to get a graduate degree so that I can either help coach executives or teach. It's a feeling that there is a higher purpose in life than just helping yourself. I am preparing myself to help others. My entire career has been a constant fire fight, at least it seems like it. I want to do more and help others.

— Shonna Andersen

———————

I have always been mission/value driven. It is vitally important to me to know that my work is to help others.

In 2019 I was diagnosed with breast cancer. When you're faced with your own mortality, you gain clarity on what is truly important. The shift for me wasn't the what (my profession). It was the how (the impact through my work). I realized that I had made a lot of sacrifices in order to be successful – including sacrificing precious time with my children, husband, friends, and community. See, the work will always be there. A company/job will take anything and everything you're willing to give it. Sure, my company cares for its employees. But the reality is that if something happened to me, while there would be sadness and perhaps a momentary sense of loss, my position would be posted the very next day. I realized that my priorities were inappropriately weighted towards my job and I hadn't treated those closest to me as a priority. I began to think about what impact I wanted to make, and the legacy I would leave. It became clear that everything – everything – is about people. To make the impact I wanted to make, I needed to first re-evaluate my (unhealthy) relationship with work. Nowhere in the agreement between myself and my employer was working 60-70+ hour weeks and sacrificing everyone who was important around me in exchange for a job well done.

I quickly began to prioritize my mental, emotional, and physical wellbeing, time with my husband and children, and investing in relationships with friends and my community. I was intentional about my boundaries – starting and ending my workday at reasonable times, and saying no when appropriate. An interesting shift occurred. I work less than I ever have in my career, but am considerably more impactful and effective. I have more to give to others. My laptop and work phone are closed/off until the next business day. (I'm not compelled to just "take a quick look" which becomes the wedge that sucks you in for hours.) I am a more present and intent listener, which in turn allows me to help others more effectively.

My mission—personally and professionally—is for every human I interact with to know: I see you. You are valued. You are cared for. You matter.

    — Kyra Matkovich

———————

I've had a great career. It's definitely not been one that has lacked in challenges, humility, and refining but I have been blessed. I wanted to be a career person my whole life. When I met my husband I told him my goal is to be 'the career woman' and I didn't see marriage or kids in my future because I just wanted to "climb the ladder." He showed me I can have both a family and a career and, thanks to him, I have both today. The turn in myself and my career came when I started mentoring others. I saw how joyous it was to build others up and help them learn and grow. I realized that I loved helping others and doing for them more than I enjoyed being the "boss." I found great reward in seeing those around me grow, develop, and even leave me to pursue higher aspirations. One of my favorite stories is about a new college graduate who was placed on my team without my input. She had zero HR knowledge or skills and she was extremely introverted. I told her I would introduce her to HR and asked her to shadow me and then do the functions she had seen me perform such as recruiting and new hire orientation. When it came time for her to start recruiting on her own, she cried because she didn't feel like she would be successful. After some hard conversations and many tears from her, she started recruiting and became a fantastic recruiter! She then tackled new hire orientation, and the tears surfaced again. We pushed through it and she did beautifully. I challenged her while coaching her and she rose to the occasion each time. She eventually left me to pursue her law degree from the University of Texas and she is now a full-time employment attorney. Her words, "You saw something in me that I never saw in myself and you brought it out," really made an impact. Since then, I've committed to giving back by mentoring and developing those around me while also humbling myself enough to learn from those I'm mentoring.

— Jill Cole

———————

I started my career as a recruiter on the vendor side. At first, I had no idea what this industry was all about and all of the complexities behind it. Also, I learned early on, that a large part of being in my industry is keeping information in confidence.

I remember working with a recent college grad candidate who wanted to go to law school and "just needed a job." She was in the process of applying to many law schools in the state and was hoping to get into one specific school that was her long shot, and her dream.

That summer I got her into a law firm to provide administrative support to a small group of attorneys. After a few weeks of working there, I received a call from one of the attorneys asking me what her goals were and suggested that she consider applying to law school. I shared the story about her wanting to be an attorney and that this was a goal she had set for herself. She shared that she was in the process of applying to law schools. The attorney shared with me that they were very involved in one of the schools to which she had applied and would offer assistance.

The summer came to an end and so did the assignment. My candidate shared that working there confirmed what she already knew, she wanted to be an attorney. We kept in touch throughout the year. One day out of the blue, she called me with an excited tone to her voice. She shared the great news that she got into her long-shot law school. I was so excited for her accomplishment.

I called the law firm where she had worked over the summer to share the great news. The attorney who answered the phone shared that they already had heard that she had gotten in, chuckled and hung up the phone.

Years later I received a call from my summer candidate. When I answered her call, she asked if I remembered her—of course I did. She shared with me that she was now an attorney and needed someone to help the firm over the summer.

When I hung up, I was reminded of the following lessons that apply to life and work:

- *Put your best foot forward every day*
- *Always share your goals and dreams with anyone who will listen*
- *Relationships take a consistent effort*
- *Be a trusted resource*
- *Pick an industry where you can make a difference.*

I enjoy being in an industry that can change a person's world and help a company at the same time all by offering and accepting a job.

— Beth Jee

———————

I must say that my journey from being driven by seeking success to striving for significance has been more of an ongoing evolution—no single moment. Rather than a specific moment, such as changing to a new lane, it is a multi-lane highway ebbing and flowing and filled with a mosaic of reflections, where I've had the privilege to work alongside and support others in their professional growth. Witnessing their journeys and contributions and being a small part of this with them has been profoundly inspiring. It is these collectively that shaped my understanding of what real significance is - contributing to the success of others.

— Adrianne Court

I was having a conversation with my mentor after reading Never Eat Alone by Keith Ferrazzi. I was trying to gather as much information from her, so that I could get that next role I wanted. One of the key points in the book is connecting others in your network and I was trying to see how it fit in my life. So, we were talking about networking and she said something like this, "You know Crystal, one of the greatest compliments you give someone is to tell their story." That has always stuck with me, I didn't know it at the time but it shifted the way I think of mentoring and networking conversations. I now approach them with: who can I connect this person with, how can I support their journey? I get really energized when I can help someone else make a connection or accelerate by telling their story.

— Crystal Nichols

When I was an individual contributor at a large company all I wanted to do was grow both personally and professionally. I saw others and wanted to aspire to be them, so I always had the ambition and knew if I was given the opportunity, I was going to exceed expectations. As I was being developed by some great mentors, I always enjoyed learning from other senior leaders. In each meeting and interaction, I was a sponge absorbing information real time. I had the privilege of taking what I thought were their best approaches, ideas, styles, and thoughts and integrate them into my unique leadership style. I can't thank everyone who had a part in this (and there were many), but it started with Martha Burger and Aubrey McClendon.

I started at the very lowest rung, so as a leader it always gave me appreciation for every level inside of the organization. In fact, I had a slightly deeper appreciation for the support teams who lived in the trenches but were critical to keep engine thriving within the overall organization. It was my role to make sure everyone understood their value and contribution. As I was progressing as a leader the switch from success to significance flipped when I became a manager back in 2003. My department was larger in head count and diverse in responsibilities. Our team was growing, I was growing, and it was important to me that others have the same opportunities I was having. During this time, it was also important to give back to the community and become more engaged in the non-profit sector. It was my duty as a person and a leader to start expanding my contributions and significance. Initially, I had to be intentional with that focus, but it was working immediately and fueled me to do more and in short order, it became natural. Employees continued to excel in their own roles and grow internally and I began doing more within my community by volunteering and serving on boards. Employees were growing and being promoted and transferred to other departments under my purview. Other department heads were proactively calling, looking for employees as we were developing them. Even though my department had over 400 employees, we only had so many growth opportunities. It was important to keep fueling that growth and retention by providing internal and external opportunities to our deserving employees. It was so rewarding to see the impact our team had on those employees and to see their growth and contribution to the enterprise for over a decade. It's also so great to see them as leaders at various companies, running their own companies and making that same impact to others as we did to them.

— Tim Denny

—————————

When I first received Bruce's manuscript for editing, little did I know the profound impact it would have on my life. About a year and a half earlier, I had been diagnosed with stage 2 breast cancer. At that time, I was working as a registered nurse, a career I had poured my heart and soul into. Before nursing, I had been a freelance writer and editor.

Following my diagnosis, I chose to step back from my nursing role to focus on self-care as I underwent treatments. During this healing period, I returned to my roots as a freelance writer and editor, not only to keep myself occupied but also to supplement my income (plus, I enjoyed it).

Meanwhile, I began to build a website, realizing a long-held dream since becoming a nurse: to educate women about menopause and other health issues. My goal was to bridge the knowledge gap in healthcare, especially in patient education. I firmly believe that with the right information, people can and will take better care of themselves.

As I delved deeper into the flaws of our healthcare system, my passion for this project grew. However, as I put the finishing touches on my website, self-doubt crept in. Questions like, "What unique insights can I offer? What if the website fails? Could this jeopardize my nursing career?" plagued my mind.

It was during this time of uncertainty that I began editing Bruce's manuscript, Drive With Purpose. His words resonated with me, inspiring me to take a leap of faith. I chose to focus on the positive 'what ifs': What if my website succeeds? What if it becomes a haven for thousands of women? What if I can make a difference by helping women learn more about their body and health?

With a launch date now set, I am bringing my dream and passion (nurseleann.com) to life. I am hopeful and excited for what lies ahead, believing firmly in the power of living a life of significance.

This journey also led me to reflect on what matters most in my life, especially my family. Facing cancer made me realize the true value of my loved ones. It also prompted me to reassess my nursing career. I realized that, despite the aspects I loved, the stress and anxiety my previous job brought me were too great a burden. I'd much rather invest my time in something that allows me to help others and that brings me joy.

Bruce's manuscript arrived at a crucial crossroads in my life. It helped me confront my inner turmoil regarding my career and encouraged me to embrace a path that aligned with my values and deep desire to help others.

— LeAnn Gerst

———————

I have always had a servant leadership style, but as I progressed in my career, my mind shifted from success to significance during my tenure at a small manufacturing company where I was hired as the HR Director. During this time, I got more involved in the local SHRM Chapter, SAHRMA, as a volunteer. While at this company, I spent 5 years volunteering on the SAHRMA Board (up to President), and at the same helping bring joy and purpose to the lives of the workers in our organization. Because this company was small, I was able to get to know every employee and ensure that their needs were taken care of. I learned much about business and relationships through volunteering with SAHRMA. By the time I moved on from the manufacturer, I was less motivated by the title and more motivated by the purpose of my next role. Most people who know me today know that my title of CHRO doesn't define me. I strive to lead by example and take care of the people in my life. Unfortunately, I found my need for significance in unhealthy work environments. If I am not making a difference, I find another way. For about a year, I was a self-employed consultant. This was a time in my life when my success was not guaranteed, and I really needed to dig deep and decide what was important to me and what value I had to share. Through this process, I learned that my relationships with others were the most significant thing in my career. My name, integrity, and reputation were everything. At the end of the day, success is different for everyone and I measure my success by the significance I have in others' lives, both at work and at home.

— Jennifer Swisher

———————

Many years ago, our company was updating our mission statement and I was involved in the process. At the time, I realized that if I could use many of the same words, phrases and intentions from my personal mission statement, my work, career and calling would all be in sync. It was so exciting to be a part of crafting this important message which completely aligned with my personal views and directives.

— Bronwyn Allen

———————

My journey as a University of Oklahoma graduate in advertising started off with venturing into pharmaceutical sales to tackle student loans. By 1995, my path shifted to the recruiting industry. My role evolved from an IT recruiter to a leader, consultant, and business owner. In 2009, amidst Twitter's rise, I launched #TalentNet Live, the first Twitter chat for recruiters. This digital forum sparked the idea of TalentNet Live, a bootstrapped conference born from our community's desire to connect beyond screens during the economic downturn of that year.

TalentNet Live quickly became a convergence point for shared experiences in the recruiting world. Many of recruiting's current thought leaders experienced their first speaking engagement at TalentNet Live. People started telling me that their lives and careers had changed for the better because of their experiences from the conference and community. The community began connecting outside of my realm, and it took on a life of its own. At that point, I knew I couldn't stop. Despite financial and logistical challenges, the impact of TalentNet Live on individuals and the industry fueled my commitment.

In 2019, SkillScout Films created a documentary about the event entitled, "A Suite at the Table," celebrating the event's 10-year anniversary. It can be found at TalentNetLive.com/documentary.

— Craig Fisher

———————

I've thought about this and honestly, I've struggled because I can't think of a singular time or moment when I made a shift from wanting success to wanting significance (i.e., getting more out of helping others). I think it's just something that's always been in me because of my parents. It's that classic servant's heart that they both had and that they instilled in me very early. We've taken cases pro bono or at no cost to help others. We don't bill at our law firm for a lot of smaller things that just feel wrong to bill for. And we believe that community service and service to others is paramount as lawyers. We're here to make the world a better place. Don't get me wrong, I have always wanted success - just like most everyone does. So, it's not that I'm some altruistic model that people should emulate or something. But I've always viewed success as a natural byproduct of significance. When you put your heart and soul into helping others, you're not only getting something out of it and filling your cup, but I truly believe that success just naturally flows from it. People want to help those that help them. So when you pour yourself into others - when you serve - people will pour themselves into you. And they'll do that through business, through contacts, through referrals, and through so much more.

— Dustin Paschal

———————

You know, there was this defining moment in my life, a real turning point, before I even kicked off my journey in Association Management. I was deep in the world of corporate banking back then. It was all about the bottom line — making money, no matter what it took. But honestly? It wore me out, and I couldn't shake this feeling of being a sell-out. My heart and head just weren't in sync.

Then, becoming a parent changed everything. It was like a spotlight was being placed directly on how out of alignment my heart and mind were. I reached a point where I was ready to do anything, anything at all, to get back to a place where I could look in the mirror and feel proud of my work and the life I was leading.

Making the decision to leave banking was huge, and I heard it from everyone. "You're making a mistake," But deep down, I knew I needed a shift, something that would let me feel like my work was making a difference, even if it was just a tiny bit. So, I took this massive leap of faith. And you know what? God has blessed my business and my life in ways I couldn't even have imagined.

Was it a smooth ride? Heck no. But was it worth it? Absolutely, yes.

— Dena Culpepper

***

I hope you've enjoyed these inspiring stories as much as I have. These narratives aren't just accounts of professional transformation; they are testaments to the power of purpose-driven living. These individuals have all discovered that the true measure of a career is not just found in accolades or achievements, but in the positive impact made on the lives of others. Their journeys remind us that when we align our work with our deepest values and commit to serving beyond ourselves, we not only elevate our careers but enrich our lives in ways we never imagined.

As you turn the page in your own career, let their stories be a catalyst for you to reflect on your path, encouraging you to embark on your own journey toward a career marked not just by success, but by lasting significance. Should our paths converge one day, I hope to hear your story!

ACKNOWLEDGEMENTS

Special thanks to everyone that has been a part of this journey. Each of you have shown me what significance looks like every day. I see your smiles, the way you lift others, your kindness, the way you connect, and your commitment to serving everyone in your path. It's inspiring and fuels me to keep driving with purpose every day to help others see limitless possibilities beyond work to have a career filled with significance. This book would not have been possible without a special community of support.

Thank you, LeAnn Gerst, for believing in my idea (once again) and framing it up to help people see it from a different lens. I am beyond grateful for your brilliant writing, ideas, countless hours of editing, and willingness to share your perspective. You are living a life of significance, my friend.

Thank you, Deanne Vick, for your inspiration, creativity, ideas, and expertise in designing this fascinating book cover. Your work is beyond exceptional, and I am grateful to you for leaning into your significance to light up the world for others to see on the journey.

Thank you, Adam Waller, for writing this brilliant foreword to "start the engine" for readers to drive with purpose. What a joy it is to have your words embedded in this book. I've enjoyed my front row seat watching your career move from success to significance, and I am beyond grateful for you sharing this masterpiece with your heart.

Thank you to those that have endorsed this book. It means more than you know, Todd Watson, Suzanne Myers, Jimmy Taylor, and Coach Mike Snyder.

Teamwork makes the dream work and what a team this is! Thank you to those that have proofread the manuscript for feedback, shared perspective in an email or text, and validated or shared ideas to help me see things differently. I am forever grateful to have you in my circle.

Special thanks to those who shared their story in the bonus chapter "Journey's from Success to Significance:" Leslie Mensching, Jeff Palkowski, Jamie Son, Shelly Mullins, Dr. Sandra Reid, Shonna Andersen, Kyra Matkovich, Jill Cole, Beth Jee, Adrianne Court, Crystal Nichols, Tim Denny, LeAnn Gerst, Jennifer Swisher, Bronwyn Allen, Craig Fisher, Dustin Paschal, and Dena Culpepper. Each of your stories inspires us to lean into a career of significance.

And to my family—thank you for listening to me talk about this message for the last year and sharing perspective to help me shape the book. It fills my heart to watch each of you drive with purpose. Each of you inspires me to be better in every area of my life and to live a life of significance. I can't wait to watch our journey ahead!

ABOUT THE AUTHOR

Bruce Waller is a relocation executive, keynote speaker, author, and podcast host. He is known as a motivational speaker and inspires attendees to 'find their lane' and 'drive with purpose' to create significance in their career. Bruce completed his 100th Keynote presentation in 2023 and continues to inspire others to become more in the workplace and in life.

As the Vice President of Corporate Relocation for The Armstrong Company in Dallas, Texas, Bruce helps HR professionals arrange employee relocation and transportation services across the US and around the world. As a volunteer leader, Bruce is a former President of The North Texas Relocation Professionals, a regional chapter for WorldwideERC, and served as President for DallasHR, the third largest SHRM Chapter in the US. Today, Bruce serves as the Assistant

State Director of Texas SHRM, a state council that serves chapters across Texas.

Bruce is the author of several books, including *Find Your Lane*, recognized by BookAuthority in 2019 as one of the best "career change" books of all time; *Milemarkers: A 5 Year Journey*; *Life in the Leadership Lane: Moving Leaders to Inspire and Change the Workplace*, and now *Drive With Purpose: Move Your Career from Success to Significance*. Bruce also writes a weekly leadership blog called *Move to Inspire* that you can subscribe to at brucewaller.com.

Bruce is the host of *Life in the Leadership Lane*, a weekly podcast where he interviews leaders making a difference in the workplace. You can find his podcast on Apple, Spotify, and other podcast platforms, including YouTube. Be sure to subscribe, post a review, and share with others.

In 2023, Bruce received the Sales Stewardship Award, UniGroup's highest honor in sales leadership, and was recognized in 2021 as one of the "Most Admired Service Providers" on The Global Mobility Top 100 list. Bruce is also a past recipient of the Texas SHRM Volunteer Leader of the Year (2021) award and served as a SHRM influencer at the National Conference in 2022.

But Bruce's most treasured achievements are the personal notes he's received that he carries around in his briefcase, mementos of his commitment to living a purpose-driven life full of significance.

Some fun facts about Bruce—he loves peanut butter, coffee, and spending time with his grandkids, Crosby and Sutton. He's also bowled ten perfect 300 games.

SOURCES

INTRODUCTION: Success vs. Significance

1. Waller, Bruce. *Find Your Lane: Change Your GPS, Change Your Career.* Bruce W. Waller, 2017.

2. Waller, Bruce. *Milemarkers: A Five Year Journey.* Bruce W. Waller, 2019.

3. Ziglar, Zig. Retrieved from BrainyQuote: https://www.brainyquote.com/quotes/zig_ziglar_381984.

CHAPTER 1: Understanding Success

1. Schweitzer, Albert. Retrieved from BrainyQuote: https://www.brainyquote.com/quotes/albert_schweitzer_155988.

2. Holtz, Lou. *Winning Every Day: The Game Plan for Success.* Harper Business, 1999.

3. Goldsmith, Marshall. *What Got You Here, Won't Get You There.* Generic, 2013.

4. "Significance." Retrieved from Google: https://www.google.com/search?q=Significance+comes+from+the+Latin+word+significare%2C+which+means+%E2%80%9Cto+signify%E2%80%9D+or+%E2%80%9Cto+mean.%E2%80%9D&rlz=1C1GCEV_enUS945US945&oq=Significance+comes+from+the+Latin+word+significare%2C+which+means+%E2%80%9Cto+signify%E2%80%9D+or+%E2%80%9Cto+mean.%E2%80%9D&gs_lcrp=EgZjaHJvbWUyBggAEEUYOdIBBzQwNWowajSoAgCwAgA&sourceid=chrome&ie=UTF-8.

5. Einstein, Albert. Retrieved from Goodreads: https://goodreads.com.

CHAPTER 2: The Pursuit of Significance

1. Maxwell, John. Retrieved from Facebook, Maxwell Leadership. May 2016.

2. Chinese Proverb. Retrieved from The Quotations Page: https://www.quotationspage.com.

3. Maxwell, Jonn. *Failing Forward* speaking engagement. 2000.

4. King Jr, Martin Luther. Retrieved from BrainyQuote: https://brainyquote.com.

5. Oleary, John. *On Fire*. Gallery Books, 2016.

6. McCormick, Elizabeth Quote "Everything you do today builds your tomorrow."

CHAPTER 3: Discovering What Matters to You

1. Jefferson, Thomas. Retrieved from BrainyQuote: https://brainyquote.com.

2. Johnson, Samuel. Retrieved from BrainyQuote: https://brainyquote.com.

3. Buffet, Warren. Retrieved from Goodreads: https://goodreads.com.

4. Waller, Bruce. *Life in the Leadership Lane*. Bruce W. Waller, 2021.

CHAPTER 4: Building a Purpose-Driven Mindset

1. Ziglar, Zig. Retrieved from Ziglar: https://ziglar.com.

2. Dweck, Carol. *Mindset: The New Psychology of Success*. Ballatine Books, 2007.

3. Itzler, Jesse. *How Far Are You Willing To Go? | 29029 Snowbasin*. YouTube, 2023. Retrieved from https://www.youtube.com/watch?v=8dExZh6F90M

4. Wright, Billie. *Life in the Leadership Lane* podcast, episode 159. 2023.

5. McLaughlin, David. *The Mindful Leader* podcast. 2022.

6. Simants, Kelly. *Life in the Leadership Lane* podcast, episode 179. 2023.

7. Michaelangelo. Retrieved from BrainyQuote: https://brainyquote.com.

CHAPTER 5: Reassessing Your Career Path

1. Einstein, Albert. Retrieved from BrainyQuote: https://brainyquote.com.

2. Link, Jim. *Life in the Leadership Lane* podcast, episode 139. 2023.

3. Covey, Stephen R. *The 7 Habits of Highly Effective People*. Free Press, 2004.

4. Walker, Andrew. *Life in the Leadership Lane* podcast, episode 84. 2021.

5. Gilliland, Steve. *Life in the Leadership Lane* podcast, episode 106. 2022.

6. Drucker, Peter. Retrieved from Goodreads: https://goodreads.com.

7. Nobel, Alfred Bernhard. Retrieved from Britannica: https://brintannica.com.

8. The Muse. 9 Famous people who will inspire you to never give up. Retrieved from: https://www.themuse.com/advice/9-famous-people-who-will-inspire-you-to-never-give-up.

9. Frankl, Viktor. Retrieved from Goodreads: https://goodreads com.

10. Emerson, Ralph Waldo. Retrieved from Goodreads: https://goodreads.com.

CHAPTER 6: Networking With Intention

1. Buffet, Warren. Retrieved from Goodreads: https://goodreads.com.

2. Valade, Kelli. *Life in the Leadership Lane* podcast, episode 156. 2023.

3. Hoffman, Reid. Retrieved from QuoteFancy: https:// quotefancy.com.

4. Allen, James. *As a Man Thinketh, Quote.* CreateSpace Independent Publishing Platform, 2014.

5. Brady, Tom. ESPN Sports Roundtable discussion. 2023.

6. Nooyi, Indra. Retrieved from BrainyQuote: https:// brainyquote.com.

7. Carnegie, Dale. *How to Win Friends & Influence People.* Pocketbooks, 1998.

CHAPTER 7: Creating Impact Through Leadership

1. Welch, Jack. Retrieved from BrainyQuote: https:// brainyquote.com.

2. Adams, John Quincy. Retrieved from Goodreads: https:// goodreads.com.

3. Bush, George W. SHRM Conference. New Orleans, June 2022

4. Beckman, Mitch. *Life in the Leadership Lane* podcast, episode 22. 2020.

5. Swanson, Leah. *Life in the Leadership Lane* podcast, episode 153. 2023.

CHAPTER 8: Overcoming Barriers to Significance

1. Carnegie, Dale. Retrieved from BrainyQuote: https://brainyquote.com.

2. Frost, Robert. Retrieved from Goodreads: https://goodreads.com.

3. Rowling, JK. Retrieved from Goodreads: https://goodreads.com.

4. Itzler, Jesse. *Living with the Monks*. Center Street, 2018.

5. Daniels, Charlie. *The Big Interview with Dan Rather*. 2014.

6. Johnson, Spencer. *Who Moved My Cheese?*. Simon & Schuster, 2009.

7. Stoops, Bob. *Life in the Leadership Lane* podcast, episode 72. 2021.

8. Mandela, Nelson. Retrieved from Goodreads: https://goodreads.com.

9. Buffet, Warren. Retrieved from Goodreads: https://goodreads.com.

10. Davis, Misti *Life in the Leadership Lane* podcast, episode 175. 2023.

CHAPTER 9: Measuring Your Significance

1. Marshall, Peter. Retrieved from BrainyQuote: https://brainyquote.com.

2. Robbins, Tony. Retrieved from Goodreads: https://goodreads.com.

3. Rezentes, Allison. *Scaling Back and Gaining Your Best Life* podcast. 2022.

4. Reynolds, Earl. *Move to Inspire* blog. Retrieved from brucewaller.com. 2016.

CHAPTER 10: The Ripple Effect

1. Teresa, Mother. Retrieved from Goodreads: https://goodreads.com.

2. Mead, Margaret. Retrieved from BrainyQuote: https://brainyquote.com.

3. Wikipedia. Damar Hamlin. Retrieved from https://en.wikipedia.org/wiki/Damar_Hamlin#:~:text=During%20a%20Monday%20Night%20Football,local%20hospital%20in%20critical%20condition.

4. Carry The Load. Retrieved from https://carrytheload.org.

5. Move for Hunger. Retrieved from https://moveforhunger.org/blog/guinness-world-records-attempt.

6. Seidens, Rory. *Life in the Leadership Lane* podcast, episode 168. 2023.

7. Parker, Sam, and Anderson, Mac. *212: The Extra Degree*. Simple Truths, LLC, 2016.

8. Mycoskie, Blake. SHRM Conference 2021. Las Vegas, NV.

CHAPTER 11: Rules of the Road

1. Jung, Carl. Quote retrieved from Goodreads: https://goodreads.com.

2. Maxwell, John. *Ethics 101: What Every Leader Needs to Know.* Center Street, 2005.

3. HR Acuity. 56 of employees witness unethical behaviors at workplace. Retrieved from https://www.hracuity.com/news/56-of-employees-witness-unethical-behavior-at-workplace/#:~:text=More%20than%2056%25%20of%20employees,won't%20be%20taken%20seriously.

4. Michigan State University Online. Common ethical issues in the workplace. Retrieved from https://www.michiganstate universityonline.com/resources/leadership/common-ethical-issues-in-the-workplace/.

5. ESPN. (2020) Timeline of Lance Armstrong's career successes, doping allegations and final collapse. Retrieved from ESPN: https://www.espn.com/olympics/cycling/story/_/id/29177227/line-lance-armstrong-career-successes-doping-allegations-final-collapse.

6. Fine, David Terry. *Untold: Operation Flagrant Foul.* Netflix, 2022.

7. Austin, Erica. *Life in the Leadership Lane* podcast, episode 160. 2023.

8. Andersen, Shonna. *Life in the Leadership Lane* podcast, episode 135. 2022.

9. Quiroga, Rosalinda. *Life in the Leadership Lane* podcast, episode 141. 2022.

10. George, Jeri. *Life in the Leadership Lane* podcast, episode 140. 2022.

CONCLUSION: Your Roadmap to Significance

1. Einstein, Albert. Quote retrieved from BrainyQuote: https://brainyquote.com.

BONUS: Journeys from Success to Significance

1. Mandela, Nelson. Quote retrieved from Nelson Mandela Foundation: https://nelsonmandela.org.

Continue the Journey...

Post a book review on Amazon to let Bruce and others know how much you enjoyed the book.

Read other books written by Bruce:
Find Your Lane: Change Your GPS and Change Your Career
https://www.amazon.com/Find-Your-Lane-Change-Career/dp/0692865632

Life in the Leadership Lane: Moving Leaders to Inspire and Change the Workplace
https://www.amazon.com/dp/0578903644/ref=sr_1_1?dchild=1&keywords=Life+in+the+Leadership+Lane+Bruce+Waller&qid=1631790922&s=books&sr=1-1

Pick up a journal to begin sharing your story:
Milemarkers: A 5 Year Journey
https://www.amazon.com/Milemarkers-Year-Journey-Bruce-Waller/dp/0578496941

Visit Bruce's website - https://brucewaller.com/:

to subscribe to Bruce's blog—*Move to Inspire*;

to book your next keynote speaker;

to relocate your team or office;

or to listen to Bruce's latest podcast.

Follow Bruce on social media:

LinkedIn https://www.linkedin.com/in/brucewaller/

Twitter https://twitter.com/BruceWaller

Facebook https://www.facebook.com/brucewwaller

Instagram https://www.instagram.com/bruceww300/

Become a fan of *Life in the Leadership Lane* podcast, available on Apple, Spotify, or your favorite podcast channel, or watch on YouTube.